BLACK&DECKER

THE COMPLETE GUIDE TO

FINISHING
BASEMENTS

Step-by-step Projects for Adding
Living Space Without Adding On

Creative Publishing
international

MINNEAPOLIS, MINNESOTA
www.creativepub.com

Creative Publishing international

Copyright © 2009
Creative Publishing international, Inc.
400 First Avenue North, Suite 300
Minneapolis, Minnesota 55401
1-800-328-0590
www.creativepub.com

Printed in Singapore

10 9 8 7 6 5 4 3 2

Library of Congress Cataloging-in-Publication Data

The complete guide to finishing basements : step-by-step projects
for adding living space without adding on.
　　p. cm. -- (The complete guide)
　At head of title: Branded by Black & Decker®
　Includes index.
　Summary: "Shows how to handle modern materials and tools to
add an extra bathroom, a family room, bedroom, home office, or
game room to basements of homes"--Provided by publisher.
　ISBN-13: 978-1-58923-454-3 (soft cover)
　ISBN-10: 1-58923-454-5 (soft cover)
　1. Basements--Remodeling--Amateurs' manuals. I. Black & Decker
Corporation (Towson, Md.) II. Title: Branded by Black & Decker. III.
Series.

　TH4816.3.B35C685 2009
　643'.5--dc22

2008045813

The Complete Guide to Finishing Basements
Created by: The Editors of Creative Publishing international, Inc., in cooperation with Black & Decker.
Black & Decker® is a trademark of The Black & Decker Corporation and is used under license.

President/CEO: Ken Fund
VP for Sales & Marketing: Kevin Hamric

Home Improvement Group

Publisher: Bryan Trandem
Managing Editor: Tracy Stanley
Senior Editor: Mark Johanson
Editor: Jennifer Gehlhar
Creative Director: Michele Lanci-Altomare
Senior Design Managers: Jon Simpson, Brad Springer
Design Manager: James Kegley
Page Layout Artist: Christopher Fayers

Lead Photographer: Joel Schnell
Photo Coordinators: Cesar Fernandez Rodriquez, Joanne Wawra
Photo Set Builder: Bryan McLain
Shop Help: Charles Boldt

Production Managers: Linda Halls, Laura Hokkanen

Contents

The Complete Guide to
Finishing Basements

Introduction

The modern basement is a far cry from the musty, low-ceilinged root cellars and cisterns carved out beneath our homes around the turn of the last century. Our seemingly unquenchable thirst for more space in our homes has caused home designers, builders, and owners to squeeze every possible square foot of living space from our houses. And this effort to maximize space has focused attention squarely on the basement. No longer the exclusive habitat of utility rooms, workshops, and the occasional bar and party room, today's basements have opened up to the full gamut of space usage. Family rooms, bedrooms, wine cellars, home gyms, home theaters, offices . . . if there is a dedicated room for doing it, you can easily find it in the basement.

During the last years of the 1990s and the first years of this century, new home construction boomed. Contractors developed new efficiencies that enabled them to erect houses with unprecedented speed so they could keep up with demand. One of these strategies was to forego time-consuming finishing where they could, and in particular in the basement. As a result, hundreds of thousands of homes were built with an unfinished basement. This was a benefit for the homebuyers as well because it shaved several thousand dollars off the construction price in a market where costs were soaring. And, being by nature ambitious, new homeowners everywhere vowed to take on the challenge of finishing their basements themselves.

If you are among the new homeowners whose basement is an empty space with a few plumbing stub-outs and little else but potential, this book is for you. In it you'll find answers to all of the questions you have undoubtedly formed as you've dreamt about the many options that await you below the grade. If you own an older house with a basement that has been finished a few decades ago but is badly in need of an update, you will also find the information you need in the pages of *The Complete Guide to Finishing Basements*. From design to planning and execution, we show you in vivid detail the steps you'll need to take to expand your living space in beautiful new ways.

When you're remodeling a house, just about everything changes once you get below ground. Most of the unique challenges found in basement building are related to water and moisture issues. But other factors come into play as well: access, ventilation, clearances, and egress are just a few of them. All of the information in this book is reported with the specific demands of basement remodeling in mind so you can be confident when using it for guidance. Creating comfortable new living space in your basement is a very rewarding way to expand the horizons of your house while adding value by increasing the assessable square footage.

REMODELING BASICS

Evaluating & Planning

Planning a basement remodeling project is a different process than planning an addition or even a routine remodeling project in the upper-level living spaces. In basements, you typically do not have the option of adding floor space, and you must confront the fact that some of the existing space may not be suitable for remodeling (no matter how much you want it to be). So to a great extent the planning process must begin with a sober evaluation of the basement. How much of the space is potentially inhabitable and how much must continue to serve a specific utility function, such as housing the furnace or the laundry machines? Will you be able to provide adequate egress (means of escape) in all areas? If not, how does that limit the kinds of rooms you may build?

In basements you will face the inevitable issue of water. Even in brand new homes, basements are more humid than the rest of the house. And the fact that you see no signs of water infiltration today does not guarantee that the floors and walls will be dry tomorrow. Do you need to consider the probability of future problems when you are selecting wall, floor, and ceiling treatments? By asking and answering these and other questions up front you can plan and design a basement remodeling project that meets your needs, satisfies local codes, and is not filled with surprises.

In this chapter:

- Basement Possibilities
- Evaluating Your Basement
- Remodeling Codes & Practices
- Planning Your Projects

Basement Possibilities

What do you want your basement to look like? Is there a missing room in your house that you've always dreamed about having? A basement bar? A family room? A guest bedroom? A wine cellar? Perhaps a home theater or a state-of the-art workshop. As long as you do the required work to make the basement space safe and comfortable, there is virtually no limit to the number of finishing possibilities. The most popular basement rooms are a family/rec room and a bedroom. With each of these, a basement bathroom is a good fit—even if it is a small half-bath.

Family rooms: Parents love basement family rooms for many reasons, chief among them that they segregate the mess and noise that tends to follow kids. If your basement has a walkout level (a very common setup), you can create an easy transition between indoor and outdoor play areas with a simple patio door. If you enjoy having friends over for backyard cookouts or to watch a ball game, a basement rec room is a perfect place, and it can usually be located with easy access to the grill. Basements tend to stay cool in the summer, which makes the family room a great place for kids to hang out on summer break. But add a gas fireplace and you can make the room a cozy gathering place in winter as well.

Bedrooms: A basement bedroom is a dream come true for many kids, especially as they enter their teens.

It offers enough distance from mom and dad yet is close enough that kids still feel secure. And if the bedroom happens to be located next to a family room with a big screen TV and full video hookups, your basement will quickly become sleepover central. A basement bedroom is also a great location for a guest bedroom, perhaps even one that does double duty as a craft room or home office.

Other rooms: Some rooms are naturally at home in a basement. This is especially true for rooms that support noisy or messy activities: a workshop, a home theater, a laundry room, or an art studio. Some rooms benefit from the relative coolness of a basement. Among them are wine cellars (with tasting tables of course), pantries, and general storage space. If you or someone in your family enjoys an activity that is high impact, finding a spot for it in the basement is a good solution for everyone. A basement gym, a practice room for the band, a dance studio, or even a metal shop all fit better in a basement environment than in other areas of your house.

Dream rooms: Basements, especially in newer homes, offer large spaces that can be claimed for big rooms. A dream spa and bath with a jetted tub and sauna; a billiards lounge, where you actually have enough room to make unobstructed shots; a home for your model railroad; a hot tub party room; the options are virtually endless.

A full kitchen in the basement is a bit unusual, but if you've always dreamt of being able to work in an Olympic-sized kitchen, you may find that an unfinished basement is the best spot to find the floor space you need. A state-of-the-art ventilation system is a crucial element if you install a kitchen underground. And unless you're intending to add a basement dining room, be sure to allocate some of the floor space for a dining table or a banquette.

A basement room doesn't have to be a room at all. Here, a quiet corner beneath a staircase is finished out to create an intimate reading and conversation spot. More of a stopping off point than a room, it nevertheless adds a new dimension to the living space in this home. It also makes use of a lovely window that's tucked in above the knee wall foundation.

A finished basement can be a single room or a whole series of rooms, as is the case with the living suite seen here. By applying the same decorative elements throughout the suite, the homeowners were able to reinforce the overall design and create a feeling of openness that carries from room to room.

A sunken feeling is a natural effect of a basement room, as in this sitting room that is very reminiscent of a 1970s-era sunken living room. Warm neutral colors and an inviting fireplace successfully fight back against the coldness that can consume a basement.

Let your imagination run wild in your basement. Your design sensibilities may be constrained by convention in the more formal areas of your house, but when you're decorating your remodeled basement, you can reach deep into your bag of design tricks and pull in the colors and styles that let you express yourself fully.

Simple as 1-2-3: excellent lighting, great acoustics, and super-comfortable seating add up to a home theater that packs 'em in every night.

A basement bathroom is a real convenience if you're adding lower level living space, such as a bedroom or family room. If you have the space and the resources to install a three-quarter bath or a full bath, you'll appreciate the added functionality. See pages 202 to 211.

Guest bedrooms are one of the most common basement remodeling projects. Often, they are designed as multipurpose rooms so, for example, you can use the room as a home office when it is not being employed as a bedroom. See pages 212 to 217.

A family room is a great addition to a basement because it keeps the rumpus and clutter and noise on its own level. A gas fireplace adds some warmth to the room. See pages 218 to 225.

An intimate wine cellar fits perfectly in a basement, (the presence of the word *cellar* in the name is a good clue). You'll want to wall off the area and appoint it with racking systems and in some cases climate control. A tasting table makes the room suitable for entertaining.

Evaluating Your Basement

Measure clearances from pipes and ductwork to walls and ceilings. Any obstructions that are not contained within the stud or joist cavities will need to be moved or isolated in framed chases or soffits.

Begin your basement evaluation by measuring from the basement floor to the bottom of the floor joists above. Most building codes require habitable rooms to have a finished ceiling height of seven and a half feet, measured from the finished floor to the lowest part of the finished ceiling. However, obstructions, such as beams, soffits, and pipes, (spaced at least four feet on center) can usually hang down six inches below that height. Hallways and bathrooms typically need at least seven-foot ceilings.

While it's impractical to add headroom in a basement, there are some ways of working around the requirements. Ducts and pipes can often be moved, and beams and other obstructions can be incorporated into walls or hidden in closets or other uninhabitable spaces. Also, some codes permit lower ceiling heights in rooms with specific purposes such as recreation rooms. If headroom is a problem, talk to the local building department before you give up on your dream room.

A well-built basement is structurally sound and provides plenty of support for finished space, but before you cover up the walls, floor, and ceiling,

check for potential problems. Inspect the masonry carefully. Large cracks may indicate a shifting around the foundation; severely bowed or out-of-plumb walls may be structurally unsound. Small cracks usually cause moisture problems rather than structural woes, but they should be sealed to prevent further cracking. Contact an engineer or foundation contractor for help with foundation problems. If you have an older home, you may find sagging floor joists overhead or rotted wood posts or beams; any defective wood framing will have to be reinforced or replaced.

Your basement's mechanicals are another important consideration. The locations of water heaters, pipes, wiring, circuit boxes, furnaces, and ductwork can have a significant impact on the cost and difficulty of your project. Can you plan around components or will they have to be moved? Is there enough headroom to install a suspended ceiling so mechanicals can remain accessible? Or, will you have to reroute pipes and ducts to increase headroom? Electricians and Heating Ventilation and Air Conditioning (HVAC) contractors can assess your systems and suggest modifications.

How to Evaluate Your Basement

Trace plumbing lines and note locations of shutoff valves on supply lines, which are natural points for adding new pipes or redirecting old pipes. If you are considering a bathroom or kitchen addition, also trace drain lines back to the main drain stack, and take measurements to determine if adding new drain lines is feasible.

Evaluate headroom in your basement, paying particular attention to ductwork that is mounted below the bottoms of the floor joists. In many cases, you can reroute the ductwork so it runs in the joist cavity.

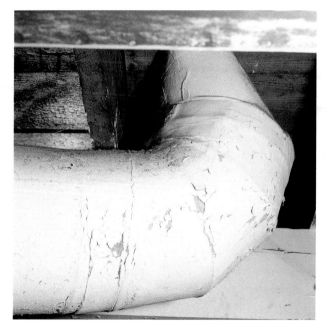

Look for asbestos insulation, usually found on hot air supply ducts from the furnace. Asbestos removal is dangerous and closely regulated, but it in many cases you can do it yourself if you follow the right proscriptions. Check with your local building department or waste management authority for more information on asbestos abatement in your area.

Identify sources of standing water and visible leaks. If water comes into the basement on a regular basis through the foundation walls or floor, you'll definitely need to correct the problem before you begin your basement project. See pages 30 to 39.

(continued)

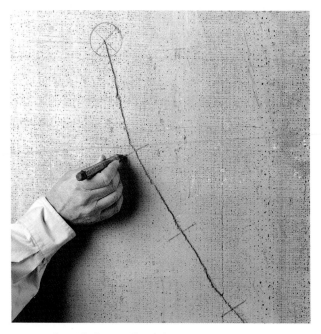

Inspect foundation wall cracks to see if they are stable. Draw marks across the crack and take measurements at the marks. Compare measurements for a few months to see if the crack is widening. If the crack is stable you can repair it (see page 30). If it is moving, contact a structural engineer and resolve the problem before you begin your remodeling project.

Probe small cracks in poured concrete walls and floors with a cold chisel to evaluate the condition of the concrete. If the concrete flakes off easily, keep probing until you get to solid concrete. If the crack and loose material extend more than 1" or so into the wall, contact a structural engineer.

Check the mortar joints on concrete block foundation walls. Some degradation is normal, but if gaps wider than ¼" have formed, you should have the wall repaired before you begin building.

Check for bowing in basement walls. Water pressure in the ground often causes concrete walls to bow inward over time. As long as the amount of bowing is less than 1 or 2" and the bowing is not active, you can usually address the problem by furring out from the wall with a framed wall.

Testing Basement Conditions

Test concrete floors for moisture seepage by taping a piece of plastic to the floor and leaving it in place for a day. If moisture is entering the basement through the floor, you will see it accumulating on the underside of the plastic.

Test concrete foundation walls for moisture and condensation. Tape a small square of aluminum foil to the wall and leave it in place for a day. If the outside surface of the foil becomes wet, you have a condensation problem, which is normally corrected by installing a dehumidifer. If the surface against the wall becomes wet, you have a seepage problem (see pages 30 to 39).

Test humidity. A relative humidity of 30 to 40% is considered ideal, but can be hard to achieve in a basement, where the naturally cooler temperatures mean that relative humidity is higher to start with. Use a hygrometer to measure relative humidity in your basement. If it is more than 50%, you will probably need to include the installation of a high-capacity dehumidifier in your remodeling plans.

Test for excessive radon. Radon is an odorless, colorless radioactive gas that can enter up through basement floors and accumulate, posing a health hazard. Some smoke detectors will detect radon, but only if it is already at dangerous levels. To determine if you have a potential radon problem, you can purchase a fairly expensive digital radon detector, or you can buy an inexpensive home detection kit available at hardware stores. You simply take an air sample with the kit collector and mail the sample to the laboratory. In most cases, you'll receive a report with recommendations in a week or two.

A new, high-efficiency water heater that's sized for your usage is a good investment.

Fuel type

Tank capacity

Working pressure

Installation clearances

Insulation R-value

Evaluate your water heater to determine if it has enough capacity to support a basement bathroom, especially if your project will include a bathtub or shower. If you already run out of hot water on occasion (or if your current water heater is more than 7 to 10 years old), consider upgrading.

Electrical Capacity ▶

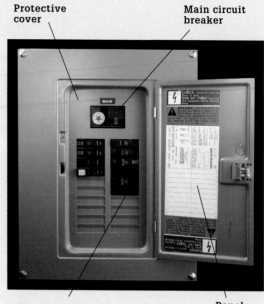

Protective cover

Main circuit breaker

Circuit breaker

Panel index

Check your main electrical service panel to gauge if there is enough available capacity for you to add the additional electrical circuits your remodeling will require. Start by looking for unused slots that are still covered with metal knockout plates. If there are several available, that's a good sign that you may be able to expand. But to know for sure, you'll need to calculate the current load your home is using and compare it to the maximum capacity. You can find the information for making these calculations in any wiring book or on the Internet. Or, have an electrician make the assessment for you. Here are general guidelines for new circuits:

Small bathroom: One 15-amp light circuit and one dedicated 20-amp small appliance circuit (GFCI protected).

Bathroom suite: One 15-amp light circuit; one 20-amp small appliance circuit (GFCI protected); dedicated 30- or 40-amp, 240-volt circuit for jetted bath or sauna; dedicated 20-amp, 240-volt circuit for electric baseboard heaters (up to 16 ft).

Bedroom: One 15-amp light circuit; One 15- or 20-amp receptacle circuit.

Home office/home theater: One 15-amp light circuit; One 20-amp receptacle circuit with surge protection; structured wiring or home networking cabling as required.

Measure the distance from areas where you are considering installing plumbing drains to the main drain stack. The new branch drain line needs to slope down to the main stack at a minimum rate of ¼" per ft. The slope is created by running the drain line through the existing floor and tying into the main stack below floor level (see pages 202 to 206) or by elevating the fixture.

Basement Construction ▸

Modern basements vary somewhat in how they are constructed, but most have concrete or concrete block foundation walls that are poured on footings and support the walls above them. The joists for the first floor are supported on the ends by sills that are fastened to the tops of the foundation walls, which they share with rim joists. The joists are usually supported in the center by a beam that is in turn supported by posts and beams or by a load-bearing wall that runs straight through the house. The bearing wall rests on an area of the floor that has been reinforced with a footing.

If the house is built on sloping terrain, it is common to have a walkout door so the basement area may be entered at grade level on the low end of the slope. In addition to making access easier, the walkout door (often a sliding patio door) allows plenty of natural light into the basement.

In some older homes, the basement foundation walls do not bear weight. You can usually identify these by the fact that the walls extend only a short distance below grade, and are often set back from a ledge of buttressed earth. In these basements, the bulk of the bearing work is done by posts and beams.

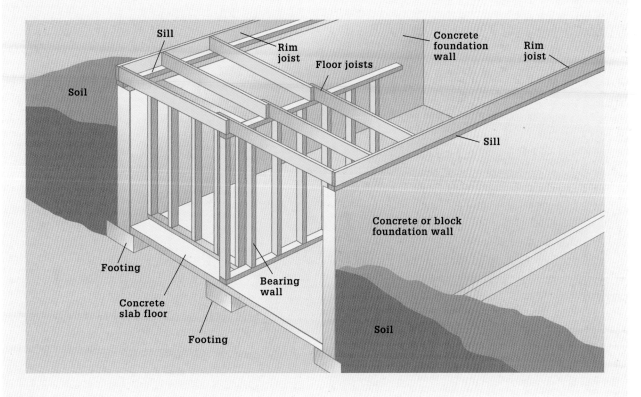

Remodeling Codes & Practices

Converting a basement into livable space involves conquering a set of challenges that are unique to subterranean construction. This is why basement remodeling and finishing is regulated with codes and practices that differ from other building. Many of the standards relate to the constant threat posed by water runoff and moisture that percolates in through the adjoining soil. Some deal with air quality in a cool environment with high relative humidity that favors mold growth. Egress (the ability to get in and out easily) is very important in basements—you can't simply jump out a window if the main entryway is blocked. Even gravity can work against you in a basement, where draining water may require assistance to be ejected efficiently.

Building codes distinguish between habitable space and nonliving space. All habitable rooms must have a footprint of at least seventy square feet (sf) with at least one wall that's seven feet or longer. The exception is a kitchen, which can be as small as fifty square feet in some instances. However, it should be noted that a small bedroom is usually considered to be in the one hundred square foot to one hundred fifty square foot range, so you should consider a seventy square foot bedroom only under extremely tight conditions. Minimum ceiling height is seven and a half feet, with some exceptions (see illustration, this page). Beams or ductwork may not drop down more than six inches from the ceiling.

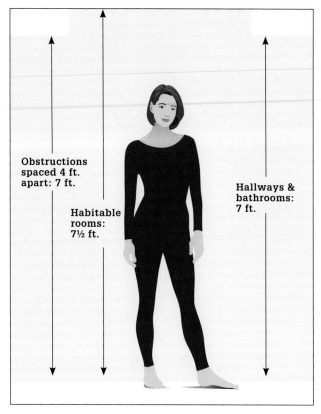

Obstructions spaced 4 ft. apart: 7 ft.

Habitable rooms: 7½ ft.

Hallways & bathrooms: 7 ft.

Basement headroom is often limited by beams, ducts, pipes, and other elements. Typical minimums for ceiling height are shown here: 7½ ft. for habitable rooms; 7 ft. for bathrooms and hallways; 7 ft. for obstructions spaced no less than 4 ft. apart.

Additional Requirements for Building in Basements ▸

Permanently installed appliances, such as furnaces and water heaters must be fully accessible for inspection, service, repair, and replacement. A dedicated furnace room must have a door at least 20" wide and large enough for passage of the furnace. There should be a minimum 30"-wide area of clear space for maintenance access. Check with your local building department for combustion air supply requirements.

Clothes dryers must exhaust to the exterior.

Bathrooms without natural ventilation must have artificial ventilation of at least 50 cu ft. per minute that is vented to the exterior. Ventilation in half baths (no tub or shower) can exhaust into the attic in some areas.

Electrical service panels may not be located in bathrooms or in closets.

GFCI receptacles or circuits are required in bathrooms, unfinished spaces, and on countertops within 6 ft. of a faucet.

Receptacles are required every 6 ft. in all habitable rooms. They are also required in any wall area wider than 2 ft., laundry areas, and in any hallway longer than 10 ft.

Habitable rooms, storage room, utility room, hallway, or staircase must have at least one switch-operated light fixture. Habitable rooms must also have an amount of window glass area equal to at least 8% of the area of the floor. At least half of the window area must be openable for unobstructed ventilation. Artificial lights and mechanical ventilation may be substituted under some conditions.

Unfinished areas must have windows with an unobstructed ventilation area equal to 1% of the floor area.

Egress Window Considerations

If your home has an unfinished or partially finished basement, it's an enticing and sensible place to expand your practical living space. Another bedroom or two, a game room, or maybe a spacious home office are all possibilities. However, unless your basement has a walk-out doorway, you'll need to add an egress window to make your new living space meet most building codes. That's because the International Residential Code (IRC) requires two forms of escape for every living space—an exit door and a window large enough for you to climb out of or for an emergency responder to enter.

Code mandates that a below-ground egress window will have a minimum opening area of at least 5.7 square feet. There are stipulations about how this open area can be proportioned: The window must be at least 20 inches wide and 24 inches high when open. Additionally, the installed window's sill height must be within 44 inches of the basement floor to permit easy escape. Typical basement windows do not meet these requirements. A large egress window requires an oversized window well. The well must be at least 36 inches wide and project 36 inches or more from the foundation. If the window well is deeper than 44 inches, it must have a fixed ladder for escape.

What does this all mean for the ambitious do-it-yourselfer? The good news is that if you've got the nerve to cut an oversized opening in your home's foundation, and you don't mind spending some quality time with a shovel, installing a basement egress window is a manageable project. Here's a case where careful planning, a building permit, and some help can save you considerable money over hiring a contractor to do the work. To see a complete step-by-step egress window and well installation, see pages 168 to 173. Contact your local building department to learn more about specific egress requirements that apply to your area.

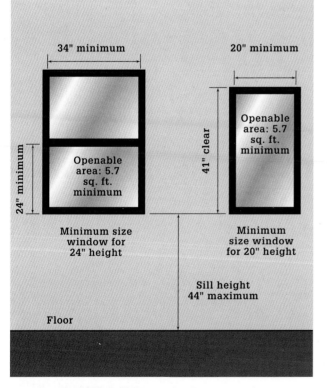

In order to satisfy building codes for egress, a basement window must have a minimum opening of 5.7 sq. ft. through one sash, with at least 20" of clear width and 24" of clear height. Casement, double-hung, and sliding window styles can be used, as long as their dimensions for width and height meet these minimum requirements.

Egress window wells must be at least 36" wide and project 36" from the foundation. Those deeper than 44" must have a means of escape, such as a tiered design that forms steps or an attached ladder. Drainage at the bottom of the well should extend down to the foundation footing drain, with pea gravel used as the drainage material.

Recommended Clearances ▸

A bathroom should be planned with enough approach space and clearance room to allow a wheelchair or walker user to enter and turn around easily. The guidelines for approach spaces and clearances shown here include some ADA guidelines and recommendations from universal design specialists.

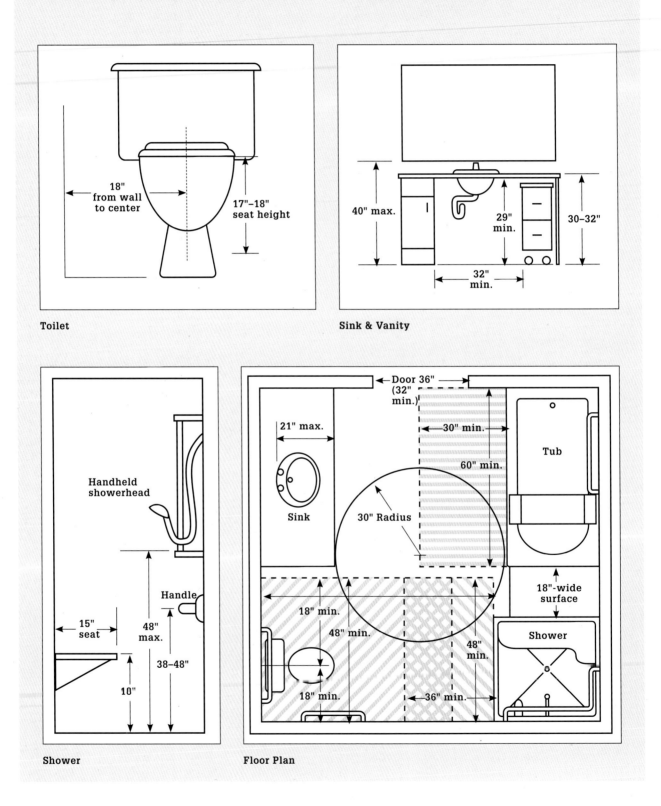

Toilet

18" from wall to center

17"–18" seat height

Sink & Vanity

40" max.

29" min.

30–32"

32" min.

Shower

Handheld showerhead

15" seat

48" max.

Handle

38–48"

10"

Floor Plan

Door 36" (32" min.)

21" max.

Sink

30" Radius

30" min.

60" min.

Tub

18"-wide surface

Shower

18" min.

48" min.

48" min.

18" min.

36" min.

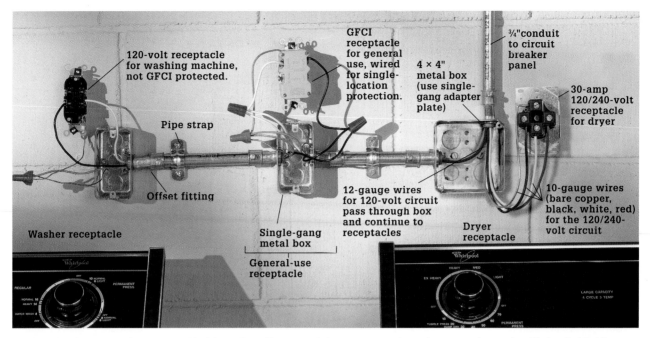

Electrical wires must be protected inside walls, ceilings, conduit, or raceway. If your basement is not classified as habitable space, you can attach sheathed electrical cable to the sides of ceiling joists, but once you've converted it to living space, all of the wiring needs to be safely tucked away.

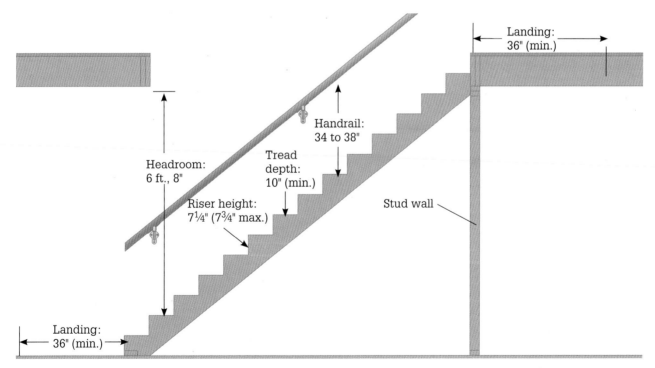

Basement stairs must be wide enough and within the allowable slope for rise and run. They also must have a grippable handrail and a clear landing area of at least 36 x 36" at both the top and bottom. They should be at least 36" wide with a minimum of 6 ft., 8" of headroom. If your house was built prior to the 1960s, there is a good chance the basement stairs don't conform to these standards (they may not even come close). Because you will be creating livable space, most municipalities will require that you upgrade or replace your stairs to meet the above requirements. Even if your local codes don't demand it, however, you should make upgrading your stairs phase one of your project anyway. Safety and convenience are reason enough.

Planning Your Project

After you've evaluated your basement and have determined that the space is usable, the next step is to plan the construction project. Having a complete construction plan enables you to view the entire project at a glance. It helps you identify potential problems, provides a sense of the time involved, and establishes a logical order of steps. Without a construction plan, it's easier to make costly errors, like closing up a wall with wallboard before the rough-ins are inspected.

The general steps shown here follow a typical construction sequence. Your plan likely will differ at several points, but thinking through each of these steps will help you create a complete schedule.

1. Contact the building department and discuss your project with a building official. Find out what codes apply in your area and how to obtain the applicable permits. Explain how much of the work you plan to do yourself. In some states, plumbing, electrical, and HVAC work must be done by licensed professionals. Also determine what types of drawings you'll need to get permits and what costs will be.

2. Design the space. Take measurements, make sketches, and test different layouts—find out what works and what doesn't. Consider all the necessary elements, such as headroom, lighting, mechanicals, and make sure everything adheres to local building codes.

3. Draw floor plans. Most basement remodels can follow a simple set of plans that you can draw yourself. Plans should include dimensions of rooms, doors, and windows; all plumbing fixtures and HVAC equipment; electrical fixtures, receptacles, and switches; and closets, counters, and other built-in features.

4. Hire contractors. If you're getting help with your project, it's best to find and hire the contractors early in the process. You may need certain contractors to pull their own permits. To avoid problems, make sure all contractors know exactly what work they are being hired to do and what work you will be doing yourself. Always check contractor's references and make sure they're licensed and insured.

5. Get the permits. Take your drawings, notes, and any required documents to the building department, and obtain the permits for your project. Find out what work needs to be inspected and when to call for inspections. This is a critical step, as the permit process is required by law.

6. Make major structural and mechanical changes. Prepare the space for finishing by completing structural work and building new stairs, if necessary. Move mechanical elements and re-route major service lines. Complete rough-ins that must happen before the framing, such as adding ducts, installing under-floor drains, and replacing old plumbing.

7. Frame the rooms. Build the floors, walls, and ceilings that establish your new rooms. In most cases, the floor will come first; however, you should rough-in service lines and insulate for soundproofing before installing the subfloor. Next come the walls. Cover foundation walls, and build partition walls and knee walls. Build the rough openings for windows and doors. Enlarge existing basement window openings or cut new ones for egress windows. Install the windows.

8. Complete the rough-ins. Run DWV (drain, waste, and vent) and water and gas supply pipes. Install electrical boxes, and run the wiring. Complete the HVAC rough-ins. Build soffits to enclose new service lines.

9. Insulate. Insulate the walls, ceilings, and pipes for weatherizing, soundproofing, and fireblocking. Add vapor barriers if required by local code.

10. Finish the walls and ceilings. If you're installing wallboard, do the ceilings first, then the walls. Tape and finish the wallboard. Install other finish treatments.

11. Add the finishing touches. Complete finish carpentry, such as installing doors, moldings and other woodwork, cabinets, and built-in shelving, and lay the floor coverings.

12. Make the final connections. Install the plumbing fixtures and complete the drain and supply hookups. Make electrical connections, and install all fixtures, devices, and appliances. Get the final inspection and approval.

Sample Basement Layout: Before and After ▶

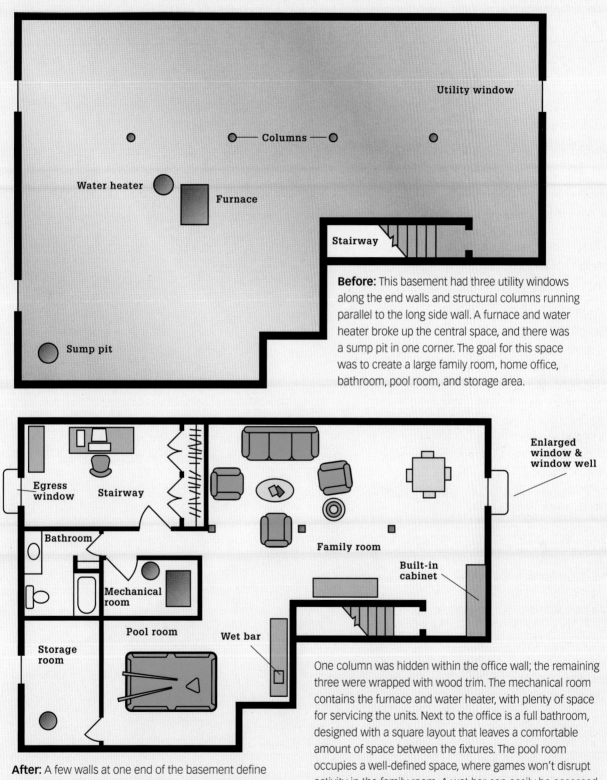

Utility window

Columns

Water heater

Furnace

Stairway

Sump pit

Before: This basement had three utility windows along the end walls and structural columns running parallel to the long side wall. A furnace and water heater broke up the central space, and there was a sump pit in one corner. The goal for this space was to create a large family room, home office, bathroom, pool room, and storage area.

Egress window

Stairway

Enlarged window & window well

Bathroom

Family room

Mechanical room

Built-in cabinet

Pool room

Wet bar

Storage room

After: A few walls at one end of the basement define several of the new rooms. To add light to the home office, the existing window opening was expanded. An egress window was installed, allowing the room to be used as a bedroom as well. A larger window and well were installed to provide light and a better view from the family room.

One column was hidden within the office wall; the remaining three were wrapped with wood trim. The mechanical room contains the furnace and water heater, with plenty of space for servicing the units. Next to the office is a full bathroom, designed with a square layout that leaves a comfortable amount of space between the fixtures. The pool room occupies a well-defined space, where games won't disrupt activity in the family room. A wet bar can easily be accessed from both the pool room and family room. The stairway needed only a new handrail to become code-compliant. At the bottom of the stairs, a built-in cabinet provides storage and adds a decorative touch to the basement entrance.

Improving Basement Environments

Before you get down to the actual building of rooms, you need to make any environmental upgrades that are necessary for the comfort, safety, and livability of the room. Now is the time to deal with water or moisture problems, heating and cooling requirements, ventilation needs, and upgrades to the wiring or plumbing systems that are needed to support additional finished living space. Ultimately, the success of your rec room or laundry room or guest bedroom depends vitally on how conscientiously you manage the environmental changes that are unique to a basement.

As you prepare the basement for construction, keep a few fundamental guidelines in mind. Each of these is addressed in greater detail in this chapter.

- Do not insulate exterior basement walls on the interior side.
- Do not install vapor barriers on the interior side of basement walls (unless required by local codes).
- Leave airspace between furred basement walls and exterior walls.
- Make sure all moisture infiltration problems are addressed by eliminating the source or, if that is not possible, by installing a sump pump or other mechanical means for removing water.

In this chapter:

- Controlling Moisture
- Controlling Pests
- Insulating Basements
- Improving Heating & Cooling
- Upgrading Ventilation
- Adding Electrical Circuits

Controlling Moisture

Basement moisture can destroy your efforts to create functional living space. Over time, even small amounts of moisture can rot framing, turn wallboard to mush, and promote the growth of mold and mildew. Before proceeding with your basement project, you must deal with any moisture issues. The good news is that moisture problems can be resolved, often very easily.

Basement moisture appears in two forms: condensation and seepage. Condensation comes from airborne water vapor that turns to water when it contacts cold surfaces. Vapor sources include humid outdoor air, poorly ventilated appliances, damp walls, and water released from concrete. Seepage is water that enters the basement by infiltrating cracks in the foundation or by leeching through masonry, which is naturally porous. Often caused by ineffective exterior drainage, seepage comes from rain or groundwater that collects around the foundation or from a rising water table.

If you have a wet basement, you'll see evidence of moisture problems. Typical signs include peeling paint, white residue on masonry (called efflorescence), mildew stains, sweaty windows and pipes, rusted appliance feet, rotted wood near the floor, buckled floor tile, and strong mildew odor.

To reduce condensation, run a high-capacity dehumidifier in the basement. Insulate cold-water pipes to prevent condensate drippage, and make sure your dryer and other appliances have vents running to the outside. Extending central air conditioning service to the basement can help reduce vapor during warm, humid months.

Crawlspaces can also promote condensation, as warm, moist air enters through vents and meets cooler interior air. Crawlspace ventilation is a source of ongoing debate, and there's no universal method that applies to all climates. It's best to ask the local building department for advice on this matter.

Solutions for preventing seepage range from simple do-it-yourself projects to expensive, professional jobs requiring excavation and foundation work. Since it's often difficult to determine the source of seeping water, it makes sense to try some common cures before calling in professional help. If the simple measures outlined here don't correct your moisture problems, you must consider more

Repairing cracks restores the integrity of concrete foundation walls that leak, but it is often only a temporary fix. Selecting an appropriate repair product and doing careful preparation will make the repair more long lasting. A hydraulic concrete repair product like the one seen here is perfect for basement wall repair because it actually hardens from contact with water.

extensive action. Serious water problems are typically handled by installing footing drains or sump pump systems. Footing drains are installed around the foundation's perimeter, near the footing, and they drain out to a distant area of the yard. These usually work in conjunction with waterproof coatings on the exterior side of the foundation walls. Sump systems use an interior underslab drainpipe to collect water in a pit, and water is ejected outside by an electric sump pump.

Installing a new drainage system is expensive and must be done properly. Adding a sump system involves breaking up the concrete floor along the basement's perimeter, digging a trench, and laying a perforated drainpipe in a bed of gravel. After the sump pit is installed, the floor is patched with new concrete. Installing a footing drain is far more complicated. This involves digging out the foundation, installing gravel and drainpipe, and waterproofing the foundation walls. A footing drain is considered a last-resort measure.

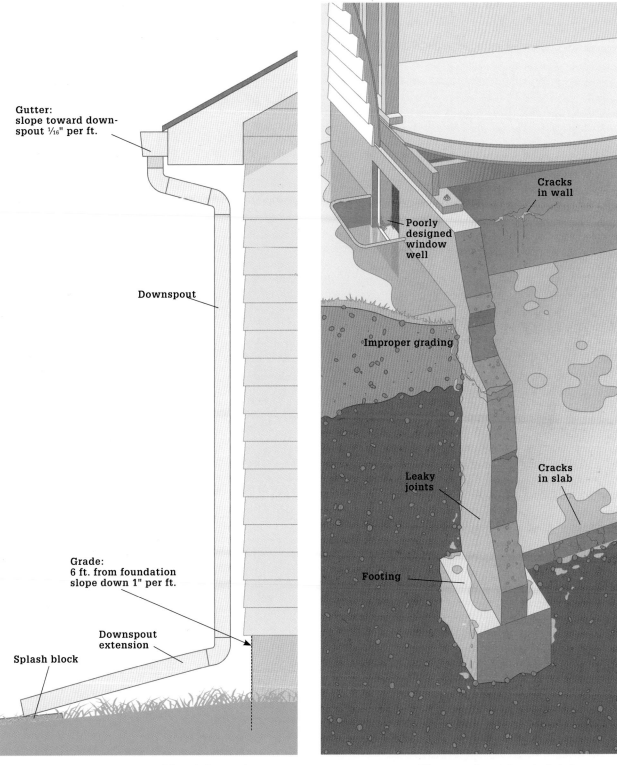

Gutter:
slope toward down-
spout ¹⁄₁₆" per ft.

Downspout

Grade:
6 ft. from foundation
slope down 1" per ft.

Downspout
extension

Splash block

Cracks
in wall

Poorly
designed
window
well

Improper grading

Cracks
in slab

Leaky
joints

Footing

Improve your gutter system and foundation grade to prevent rainwater and snowmelt from flooding your basement. Keep gutters clean and straight. Make sure there's a downspout for every 50 ft. of roof eave, and extend downspouts at least 8 ft. from the foundation. Build up the grade around the foundation so that it carries water away from the house.

Common causes of basement moisture include improper grading around the foundation, inadequate or faulty gutter systems, condensation, cracks in foundation walls, leaky joints between structural elements, and poorly designed window wells. More extensive problems include large cracks in the foundation, damaged or missing drain tiles, a high water table, or the presence of underground streams. Often, a combination of factors is at fault.

How to Seal Cracks in a Foundation Wall

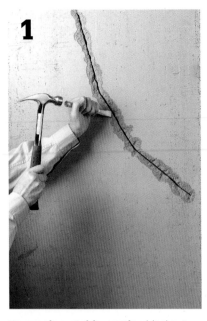

1

2

3

To repair a stable crack, chisel cut a keyhole cut that's wider at the base then at the surface, and no more than ½" deep. Clean out the crack with a wire brush.

To help seal against moisture, fill the crack with expanding insulating foam, working from bottom to top.

Mix hydraulic cement according to the manufacturer's instructions, then trowel it into the crack, working from the bottom to top. Apply cement in layers no more than ¼" thick, until the patch is slightly higher than the surrounding area. Feather cement with the trowel until it's even with the surface. Allow to dry thoroughly.

How to Skim-Coat a Foundation Wall

1

2

Resurface heavily cracked masonry walls with a water-resistant masonry coating such as surface bonding cement. Clean and dampen the walls according to the coating manufacturer's instructions, then fill large cracks and holes with the coating. Finally, plaster a ¼" layer of the coating on the walls using a square-end trowel. Specially formulated heavy-duty masonry coatings are available for very damp conditions.

Scratch the surface with a paintbrush cleaner or a homemade scratching tool after the coating has set up for several hours. After 24 hours, apply a second, smooth coat. Mist the wall twice a day for three days as the coating cures.

Preventing Moisture in Basements

Waterproof Paint ▸

Masonry paints and sealers, especially those that are described as waterproof, are rather controversial products. Some manufacturers claim that applying a coat of their waterproof paint will create a seal that can hold back moisture, even under light hydrostatic pressure. Others suggest only that their product, when applied to a basement wall, will create a skin that inhibits water penetration from the interior side.

Masonry paints do hold up better on concrete surfaces than other types, largely because they are higher in alkali and therefore less reactive with cement-based materials. But they also can trap moisture in the concrete, which will cause the paint to fail prematurely and can cause the concrete to degrade, especially if the water freezes. Read the product label carefully before applying waterproof paint to your basement walls, and make sure to follow the preparation protocols carefully. If you have a foundation wall with an active water-seepage problem, address the problem with the other methods shown in this section, including grading and gutters. A coat of waterproof paint is not going to make your basement drier.

Clean your gutters and patch any holes. Make sure the gutters slope toward the downspouts at about 1/16" per ft. Add downspout extensions and splash blocks to keep roof runoff at least 8 ft. away from the foundation.

Cover window wells that will otherwise allow water into a basement. Covering them with removable plastic is the easiest way to keep them dry. Covers on egress window wells must be easily removed from inside (see page 168). If you prefer to leave wells uncovered, add a gravel layer and a drain to the bottom of the well. Clean the well regularly to remove moisture-heavy debris.

Drainage Solution: How to Re-grade

Establish the drainage slope. The yard around your house should slant away from the house at a minimum slope of ¾" per ft. for at least 10 ft. Till the soil or add new soil around the house perimeter. Drive a wood stake next to the house and another 10 ft. out. Tie a level mason's string between the stakes, and then move the string down at least 2½" at the end away from the house, establishing your minimum slope.

Redistribute the soil with a steel garden rake so the grade follows the slope line. Add topsoil at the high end if needed. Do not excavate near the end of the slope to accommodate the grade. The goal is to build up the yard to create runoff.

Use a grading rake to smooth out the soil so it slopes at an even rate. Drive additional stakes and tie off slope lines as necessary.

Tamp the soil with a hand tamper or plate compactor. Fill in any dips that occur with fresh dirt. Lay sod or plant grass or groundcover immediately.

Dry Wells for Drainage ▸

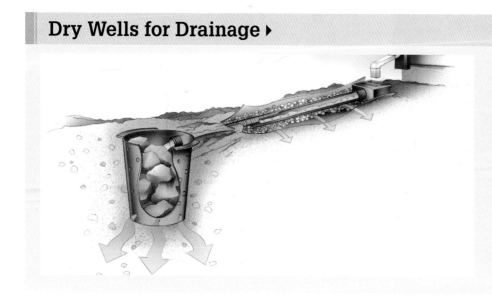

A dry well is installed to help give runoff water an escape route so it doesn't collect around the house foundation. See next page.

Drainage Solution: How to Install a Dry Well

A dry well is a simple way to channel excess water out of low-lying or water-laden areas, such as the ground beneath a gutter downspout. A dry well system (see previous page) typically consists of a buried drain tile running from a catch basin positioned at the problem spot to a collection container some distance away.

A dry well system is easy to install and surprisingly inexpensive. In the project shown here, a perforated plastic drain tile carries water from a catch basin to a dry well fashioned from a plastic trash can, that has been punctured, then filled with stone rubble. The runoff water percolates into the soil as it makes its way along the drainpipe and through the dry well.

The how-to steps of this project include digging the trench with a shovel. If the catch basin is a long distance from the problem area, you may want to rent a trencher to dig the trench quickly. Call local utility companies to mark the location of underground mechanicals before you start to dig.

Dig a trench (10" wide, 14" deep) from the area where the water collects to the catch basin location, sloping the trench 2" per 8 ft. Line the trench with landscape fabric and then add a 1" layer of gravel on top of the fabric.

Set a length of perforated drain tile on the gravel running the full length of the trench. If the trench starts at a downspout, position a grated catch basin directly beneath the downspout and attach the end of the drain tile to the outlet port.

Install the dry well by digging a hole that's big enough to hold a plastic trash can. Drill 1" holes through the sides and bottom of the can every 4 to 6". Also cut an access hole at the top of the can for the drain tile. Set the can in the hole and insert the free end of the tile. Backfill dirt over the tile and trench and plant grass or cover with sod.

Drainage Solution: How to Build a Dry Streambed

A dry streambed or watercourse (also known as an arroyo) can be built to direct water runoff away from your house foundation and toward areas where the water can percolate into the ground and irrigate plants. When designing your dry streambed, keep it natural and practical. Use local stone that's arranged as it would be found in a natural stream. Take a field trip to an area containing natural streams and make some observations. Note how quickly the water depth drops at the outside of bends, where only larger stones can withstand the current. By the same token, note how gradually the water level drops at the inside of broad bends, where water movement is slow. Place smaller river-rock gravel here as though it had accumulated in a natural stream.

Large heavy stones with flat tops may serve as steppingstones, creating paths to cross or even follow dry stream beds.

The most important design principle for dry streambeds is to avoid regularity. Stones are never spaced evenly in nature nor should they be in your streambed. Also, if you dig a bed with consistent width it will look like a canal or a drainage ditch, not a stream, so vary the width and the depth. Consider other yard elements and furnishings. For example, a dry streambed is essentially a river of rock, so it presents a nice opportunity to add a landscape bridge or two to your yard.

Contact your local building department before deliberately routing water toward a storm sewer; this may be illegal. Before digging, call your local utilities hotline to have buried pipes and wires in or near the construction area flagged.

Tools & Materials ▸

Spades
Garden rake
Wheelbarrow
Landscape fabric
6-mil black plastic
¾ to 2" river rock

6 to 18"- dia.
  river-rock boulders
8"-thick stepping stones
Native grasses or other
  perennials for banks

A dry streambed can be constructed to direct water runoff away from your basement walls and to add an attractive landscape feature to your yard.

Excavate the streambed to about 12" deep, working within a nonregular outline. The streambed should originate at a downspout from your gutter system. Follow the natural course of rainwater runoff where possible. End at a natural sink, such as a rain garden. Bends are often wider in natural streams, so make your stream wider at bends. Rake, smooth, and compact the soil within the project area.

Lay strips of landscape fabric over the excavation area, overlapping fabric by at least 12" at seams. Lay the fabric to within 2 to 3 ft. of the house, and then lay a strip of 6-mil black plastic next to the house to direct water away and into the streambed. Weigh down the edges of the fabric with some of your larger rocks.

Place rocks in the streambed, beginning with larger boulders along the streambed banks. Extra excavation may be needed to properly set extra large boulders. Fill around large boulders and line "rapids" with smaller boulders. You may also place stepping stones to make a pathway or bridge in an area where you're likely to be walking. In most cases this feature is mostly ornamental.

Fill in spaces and create gravel bottoms with river rock in the ¾ to 2" size range. Make sure the river rock you're using is native to your area, and avoid dumping it all into a flat field. Retain some nice shapes and contours. Trim off any exposed landscape fabric and plant native grasses and other perennials along the banks (inset).

Drainage Solution: How to Make a Foundation Drainage Garden

If your basement is perpetually wet, a bit of landscaping may solve your water problem. A foundation drainage garden has dual functions of enhancing your landscape and keeping your basement dry. Check the slope of the ground near your foundation walls using a level that's set on top of a long straight 2 × 4. A minimum slope of ½" per foot is necessary for water runoff. If your slope does not meet this minimum, you'll need to regrade and add soil until the slope is achieved. When the regrading is done and sufficient slope has been established, you can install a drainage garden over a waterproof membrane. Consisting of a waterproof underlayment covered with soil or rocks (or some combination of the two), drainage gardens have the added bonus of being virtually maintenance free. It is recommended, however, that you add plant cover for visual appeal and to prevent the soil from eroding.

When selecting a material for top-dressing the drainage garden, look for colors and textures that are native to your area and probably already exist in your yard. Mulch, bark, and other organic materials do not work as dressing for foundation gardens. They will simply wash away. Similarly, very small aggregate and gravel have a way of disappearing. Crushed aggregate, river rock, or field stone in the two-inch average diameter range is an excellent choice.

Tools & Materials ▸

Excavating tools	Chalk line
Folding rule	Edging spikes
Garden rake	Gravel
Grease pencil	Hose
Hand maul	Landscape edging
Hand tamper	Landscape marking
Lawn roller	paint
Level	Perennials
Mason's string	Spun bonded
Rototiller	landscape fabric
Spade	Stakes
Utility knife	Straight 2 × 4
6-mil black plastic	

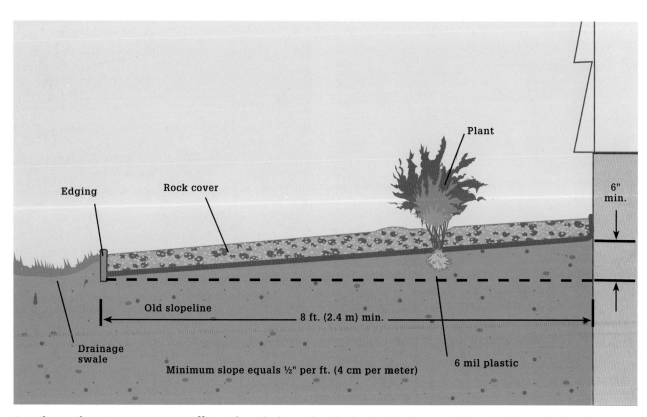

A pathway that steers water runoff away from the house, keeping it out of the basement, is created by crushed rock groundcover laid over a plastic water barrier.

Using an 8-ft.-long 2 × 4 with a level on top, mark where the grade needs to fall at the house in order to produce a minimum 4" drop from the house to a point 8 ft. away. Repeat the procedure every 10 ft. along the foundation wall. Connect the grade points with snapped chalk lines. Clear all plantings, landscape rock, landscape fabric, and other debris from the construction site.

Dig out a trench along the lower edge of the garden area, tossing the soil back toward the high end of the garden to begin the regrading work. Relocate and add soil as necessary until the minimum slope is achieved. Tamp the soil with a hand tamper or roll with a lawn roller.

Install landscape edging (inset photo), and then lay two layers of 6-mil black plastic over the excavated area, running the plastic up the wall slightly. Sheet plastic comes in wide enough rolls that you should be able to install seamless layers.

Plant hardy perennials or evergreens and then pour a 2 to 4" layer of crushed rock or gravel in the foundation garden. When planting, cut an X into the sheeting layers and build up the soil in front of the hole (underneath the plastic) to create a small dam that will help retain water for the plant. Smooth out the rock with a garden rake oriented upside down so the tines don't puncture the plastic sheeting.

Drainage Solution: How to Install a Sump Pump

If water continues to accumulate in your basement despite all your efforts at regrading and sealing your basement walls, installing a sump pump may be your only option for resolving the problem. Permanently located in a pit that you dig beneath your basement floor, the sump pump automatically kicks in whenever enough water accumulates in the pit to trigger the pump float. The water is then pumped out of the basement through a pipe that runs through the rim joist of the house.

Because you'll be digging well beneath the basement floor, make certain there is no sewer pipe or water supply pipe in the digging area. Contact a plumber if you do not know for sure that the area is clear.

The purpose of a sump pump is to collect and eject water that accumulates beneath your basement floor (usually due to a high water table) before it can be drawn or forced up into the basement. The most effective sump installations have drain tile running around the entire perimeter of the house and channeling water to the pump pit. This system can be created as a retrofit job, but it is a major undertaking best left to a pro.

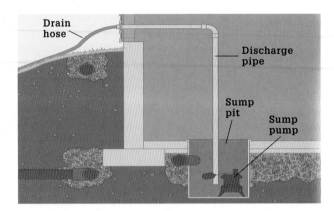

A submersible sump pump is installed in a pit beneath a basement floor to pump water out before it seeps up into the basement.

How to Install a Sump Pump

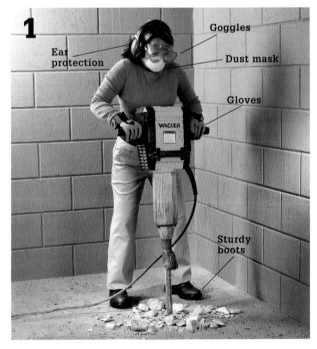

Dig the sump pit. Start by finding the lowest point of the floor (or the spot where water typically accumulates) that is at least 8" from a foundation wall. Outline an area that's about 6" wider than the pit liner all around. Remove the concrete in this area. Basement floors are typically 3 to 4" thick, so renting an electric jackhammer is a good idea.

Install the pit liner after digging a hole for it in the granular material under the floor. The hole should be a few inches wider than the liner. Remove the excavated material right away. Add gravel to the bottom of the hole as needed to bring the liner level with the top of its rim at floor level.

3

Pack the liner in place by pouring ½" gravel around it. Add a 1" base of gravel and then mix concrete to patch the floor. Trowel the concrete around the rim with a float so the patch is level and smooth.

4

Prepare the sump pump for installation. Thread a PVC adapter fitting onto the pump outlet, and then solvent glue a PVC standpipe to the adapter. The standpipe should be long enough to extend about 1 ft. past the liner rim when the pump is set on the bottom of the liner.

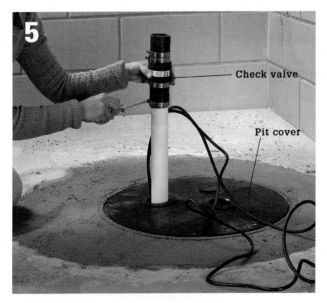

5

Check valve

Pit cover

Attach a check valve to the top of the standpipe to prevent the backflow of water into the pump pit. Solvent weld another riser to fit into the top of the check valve and run upward to a point level with the rim joist, where the discharge tube will exit the basement.

6

Drill a hole in the rim joist for the discharge tube and finish routing the drainpipe out through the rim joist. Caulk around the tube on both the interior and exterior sides. On the exterior, attach an elbow fitting to the discharge tube and run drainpipe down from the elbow. Place a splash block beneath the drainpipe to direct water away from the house. Plug the pump in to a GFCI-protected receptacle.

Controlling Pests

A typical basement offers everything a pest could ask for: it's cool and damp with plenty of hiding places and ample food sources. Insects will happily invade your basement in just about any climate, typically entering through cracks in the foundation wall as well as through floor drains. In some areas, snakes are drawn to the cool climate in basements. Other invaders include vermin (mice and rats) and, perhaps the most destructive of all, termites.

The most common entry points for vermin are small holes along the foundation and sometimes next to windows and doors. These should all be filled with silicone acrylic caulk. Holes much wider than one quarter inch should be stuffed with caulk backer before caulking. Also fill any gaps where phone, gas, cable, electric, water, and other services enter the house through the basement. Once you are done filling the obvious gaps, look for evidence of infestation like animal droppings or nesting materials. Remove these and check the area for any entry points that you might have missed. If the rodents persist, you can fight back with spring-loaded traps or Havahart-type traps that capture the animal so it can be released outside.

There are many hardware store products designed to help you get rid of pests inside your house. For insects in the basement, pesticide foggers are one option. These shouldn't be used around food prep areas or when anyone is in the house. The usual approach is to activate the fogger and then leave the house for a few hours. No matter which product you buy, follow the use instructions carefully.

Common roach and ant traps do capture a lot of pests but will not solve the problem unless the source from outside is eliminated. The same is true of mousetraps. If you've closed all the entry points that you can find, and you've trapped all the pests that were inside when you plugged the holes and you still have pests, then you need further help. Call a reputable exterminator.

If you have a termite problem, do not fool around with home remedies. Contact a pest control professional, who will most likely get you set up with a monitored trap system. Because termites can destroy your house (and new, more destructive breeds are proliferating quickly), don't take any chances.

Control termites by having a professionally monitored bait system installed. If you live in an area where termites are a problem, relying on home remedies is a risky gamble.

Use an annual perimeter spray to control insects such as silverfish and ants. Granular products also may be sprinkled around the foundation wall on the exterior side.

Pestproofing Basements

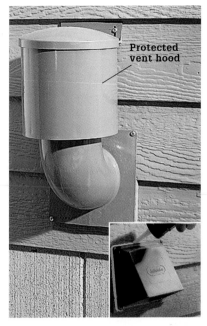

Seal the mudsill by applying caulk or expandable foam between the mudsill and the top of the foundation wall on the interior side (left photo). This is a prime entry point for crawling insects. Also check the sill area on the exterior side. Often, this is concealed by siding, but if you see any gaps fill them with caulk as well (right photo).

Caulk around dryer vents to keep pests (and water) out of the basement. For maximum protection, replace your flap-style vent outlets (inset) with a protected vent hood that keeps insects and rodents out (the warm, moist air in a dryer vent is very attractive to pests).

Protected vent hood

Block basement floor drains from becoming entry points by setting a tennis ball in the drain opening. The lightweight ball will cover the opening but float up enough to allow water to drain.

Keep an eye out for signs of pest infestation. Hills, tunnels, and droppings are all sure signs that you've got a pest problem.

Insulating Basements

Insulating basements is a tricky topic. In colder climates, insulation is necessary for the successful creation of a livable basement room. But the practice is fraught with pitfalls that can cause a host of problems. But here are two pieces of advice that are certain:

- The exterior wall is a far better location for new insulation than the interior foundation walls.
- Never insulate a wall that is not dry and well drained.

Almost all of the issues surrounding basement wall insulation have to do with moisture and water vapor. How these issues affect your plans will depend a great deal on your climate, as well as on the specific characteristics of your house, your building site, and whether or not your home was built with foundation drains and a pumping system.

Until recently, basements most often were insulated from the inside because it is easier, faster, and cheaper. A typical installation would be to attach furring strips (2 × 2, 2 × 3, or 2 × 4) to the foundation wall at standard wall stud spacing, and then fill in between the strips with fiberglass insulation batts. A sheet plastic vapor barrier would then be stapled over the insulated wall prior to hanging wallcoverings (usually wallboard or paneling). Experience has shown this model to be a poor method, very frequently leading to moisture buildup within the wall that encourages mold growth and has a negative impact on the indoor air quality. The building materials also tend to fail prematurely from the sustained moisture presence.

If your basement plans require that you insulate the foundation walls, make certain that the walls are dry and that any moisture problems are corrected (see previous section). Then, look first at the exterior.

Install insulation on the exterior of the wall, not the interior, whenever possible. Exterior insulation results in a warm wall that will have less of a problem with condensation. The wall also can breathe and dry out more easily if the interior side has no vapor retarder.

Because it is often unnecessary to insulate the full height of the wall, you may find that an exterior apron insulating approach is easier than you imagined (see pages 44 to 45). If your circumstances absolutely require that you insulate inside, use insulating products such as extruded polystyrene or foil-faced isocyanurate that do not absorb water or provide food for mold. You should also keep the wall isolated from the insulation: attach the insulation first, seal it, and then construct a stud wall that has no direct contact with the concrete or concrete block wall (see pages 46 to 47).

High-Efficiency Upgrades ▸

Replace old gas water heaters with high-efficiency models. Not only will this save money on your utilities bill, it will also keep your basement warmer. The more efficient your heater is, the less air it will require for fuel combustion, which means less fresh cold air is drawn into the basement to replace the air consumed by the appliance.

How to Insulate Basements

Install rigid foam insulation in basements, both on the exterior and the interior. Extruded polystyrene (sometimes called beadboard) is an economical choice for larger areas, and it forms its own vapor retarding layer when properly installed and sealed. High-density polystyrene and isocyanruate are denser insulation boards with higher R-values. Isocyanurate usually has one or two foil faces. It is used to seal rim joists but is a good choice for any basement wall location.

Improve insulation and thermal seals in attics and other parts of your house to keep basements warmer in winter. By reducing the amount of warm air that escapes through the roof, you will reduce the amount of cold air that is drawn in through the basement walls to replace the air.

Seal furnace ducts to reduce air leakage. Use a combination of UL 181-rated duct tape (foil tape) and duct mastic. If cold-air return ducts leak, for example, they will draw air from the basement into the air supply system. As with heat loss through the attic, this will cause fresh cold air to enter the basement and lower the ambient temperature.

What is a Dry Wall ▶

When building experts warn never to insulate a wall that isn't dry, they have something very specific in mind. A wall that appears dry to the touch may not be classified as dry if it is constantly evaporating small amounts of moisture that will be blocked if you install any kind of vapor retarder (as is likely the case). A dry wall (suitable for interior insulation) is one that is superficially dry to the touch and also meets these criteria:

- Has a positive drainage system capable of removing water that accumulates from any source (this is typically in the form of a sump pump).
- The foundation wall and floor are structured to provide drainage of water away from the house, often through the use of drain tiles and footing drains.

Insulation Solution: Exterior Apron Insulation

Insulate foundation walls on the exterior side (and not the interior) whenever you can. The easiest way to accomplish this is by installing insulation in the apron area only, so you do not have to excavate all the way to the bottom of the wall. By adding a layer of horizontal insulation in the bottom of the trench, you can realize at least 70 percent of the energy savings of insulating the whole wall, while limiting your digging to 18 inches down and 24 inches out.

Because you will be adding width to the foundation wall by installing exterior insulation, you will need to install flashing to cover the top of the insulation layer and whatever protective wall surface you cover it with. For the project shown here, the insulation is covered with panelized veneer siding over one-inch-thick rigid foam insulation boards. For extra protection, coat the cleaned walls with a layer of bituminous coating before installing the insulation boards.

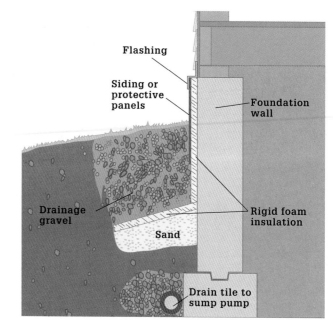

Apron insulation is an easy and effective way to enhance comfort in your basement without causing any major moisture issues.

How to Install Apron Insulation

Dig an 18 × 24" wide trench next to the wall being insulated. Make sure to have your local utilities company flag any lines that may be in the area first.

Coat the wall with a layer of bituminous coating once you have cleaned it with a hose or pressure washer. The coating simply creates another layer of moisture protection for the basement and can be skipped if you wish.

Line the trench with a 2"-thick layer of coarse sand, and then strips of rigid foam insulation. The sand should slope away from the house slightly, and the insulation strips should butt up against the foundation wall.

Install drip edge flashing to protect the tops of the insulation board and new siding. Pry back the bottom edge of the siding slightly and slip the flashing flange up underneath the siding. The flashing should extend out far enough to cover both layers of new material (at least 1½ to 2").

Bond strips of rigid foam insulation board to the foundation wall using a panel adhesive that is compatible with foam. Press the tops of the boards up against the drip edge flashing. When all the boards are installed, tape over butted seams with insulation tape.

Install siding or another protective layer over the insulation. Here, 2 x 4 ft. faux stone panels are being used. Once the panels are in place, backfill the trench with dirt or gravel. Make sure to maintain minimum slopes for runoff at grade.

Insulation Solution for Dry Walls: Interior Wall Insulation

As a general rule, avoid insulating the interior side of your basement walls. It is best to leave breathing space for the concrete or block so moisture that enters through the walls is not trapped. If your exterior basement walls meet the definition of a dry wall (see page 43) however, adding some interior insulation can increase the comfort level in your basement. If you are building a stud wall for hanging wallcovering materials, you can insulate between the studs with rigid foam—do not use fiberglass batts and do not install a vapor barrier. If you are building a stud wall, it's a good idea to keep the wall away from the basement wall so there is an air channel between the two.

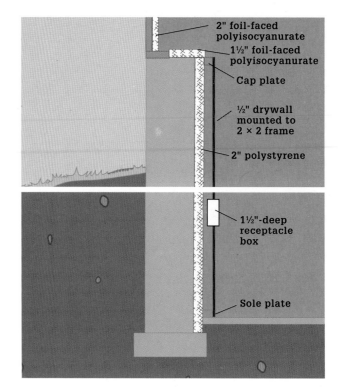

Interior insulation can be installed if your foundation walls meet the conditions for dry walls (see page 43). It is important to keep the framed wall isolated from the basement wall with a seamless layer of rigid insulation board.

How to Insulate an Interior Basement Wall

1

Begin on the exterior wall by digging a trench and installing a 2"-thick rigid foam insulation board up to the bottom of the siding and down at least 6" below grade. The main purpose of this insulation is to inhibit convection and air transfer in the wall above grade. See pages 44 to 45 for more information on how to use flashing and siding to conceal and protect the insulation board.

2

Insulate the rim joist with strips of 2"-thick isocyanurate rigid insulation with foil facing. Be sure the insulation you purchase is rated for interior exposure (exterior products can produce bad vapors). Use adhesive to bond the insulation to the rim joist, and then caulk around all the edges with acoustic sealant.

3

Seal and insulate the top of the foundation wall, if it is exposed, with strips of 1½"-thick, foil-faced isocyanurate insulation. Install the strips using the same type of adhesive and caulk you used for the rim joist insulation.

4

Attach sheets of 2"-thick extruded polystyrene insulation to the wall from the floor to the top of the wall. Make sure to clean the wall thoroughly and let it dry completely before installing the insulation.

5

Seal the gaps between the insulation boards with insulation vapor barrier tape. Do not caulk gaps between the insulation boards and the floor.

6

Install a stud wall by fastening the cap plate to the ceiling joists and the sole plate to the floor. If you have space, allow an air channel between the studs and the insulation. Do not install a vapor barrier.

Improving Heating & Cooling

Finishing a basement almost always requires that you expand your home heating system to heat the new space or add a supplementary heat source, such as electric baseboard heaters. Of these two options, installing baseboard heaters is an easier DIY project that won't compromise your existing heating. But in the right situation, extending ductwork in a forced air system to the new space may be a feasible project. In most cases, extending your current heating system will be a cheaper alternative in the long run since gas tends to be a cheaper fuel than electricity (although increases in natural gas and heating oil prices have narrowed the price gap considerably).

Although the actual work may not be difficult, you should consult a heating and cooling professional before you decide to extend your furnace heat yourself. Home heating systems are delicately balanced, and making alterations may have ramifications throughout the system that result in your furnace becoming overworked or other areas of your house being underserved. Remodeling can also create changes in your basement that impede the supply of fresh air to your furnace, so be sure to note the furnace location on your plans when you apply for a building permit.

Installing baseboard heaters is a good DIY solution for heating a basement room. They are inexpensive and relatively easy to install, and they will not impact your current home heating system.

Extending your ductwork to provide heat to a basement room is fairly easy, as long as you have access to the top of the rectangular air supply duct and there is a joist cavity in the project area for running new ductwork. But be sure to check with a contractor or inspector to make sure your system can handle the extra demands.

Heating Solution: Install Baseboard Heaters

Baseboard heaters are a popular way to provide additional heating for an existing room or primary heat to a converted basement.

Heaters are generally wired on a dedicated 240-volt circuit controlled by a thermostat. Several heaters can be wired in parallel and controlled by a single thermostat.

Baseboard heaters are generally surface mounted without boxes, so in a remodeling situation, you only need to run cables. Be sure to mark cable locations on the floor before installing drywall. Retrofit installations are also not difficult. You can remove existing baseboard and run new cable in the space behind.

Tools & Materials ▸

Drill/driver
Wire stripper
Cable ripper
Wallboard saw
Baseboard heater or heaters
Thermostat (in-heater or in-wall)
12/2 NM cable
Electrical tape
Basic wiring supplies
Flathead screws
Combination tool

How Much Heater Do You Need? ▸

If you don't mind doing a little math, determining how many lineal feet of baseboard heater a room requires is not hard.

1. Measure the area of the room in sq ft. (length × width): _____
2. Divide the area by 10 to get the baseline minimum wattage: _____
3. Add 5% for each newer window or 10% for each older window: _____
4. Add 10% for each exterior wall in the room: _____
5. Add 10% for each exterior door: _____
6. Add 10% if the space below is not insulated: _____
7. Add 20% if the space above is not well insulated: _____
8. Add 10% if ceiling is more than 8 ft. high: _____
9. Total of the baseline wattage plus all additions: _____
10. Divide this number by 250 (the wattage produced per ft. of standard baseboard heater): _____
11. Round up to a whole number. This is the minimum number of feet of heater you need. _____

Note: It is much better to have more feet of heater than is required than fewer. Having more footage of heater does not consume more energy; it does allow the heaters to work more efficiently.

Planning Tips for Baseboard Heaters ▸

- 240-volt heaters are much more energy efficient than 120-volt heaters.
- Baseboard heaters require a dedicated circuit. A 20-amp, 240-volt circuit of 12-gauge copper wire will power up to 16 ft. of heater.
- Do not install a heater beneath a wall receptacle. Cords hanging down from the receptacle are a fire hazard.
- Do not mount heaters directly on the floor. You should maintain at least 1" of clear space between the baseboard heater and the floor covering.
- Installing heaters directly beneath windows is a good practice.
- Locate wall thermostats on interior walls only, and do not install directly above a heat source.

How to Install a 240-volt Baseboard Heater

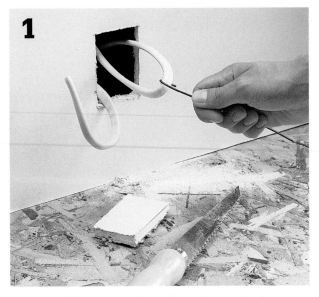

1

Cut a small hole in the drywall 3 to 4" above the floor at heater locations. Pull 12/2 NM cables through the first hole: one from the thermostat, the other to the next heater. Pull all the cables for subsequent heaters. Middle-of-run heaters will have two cables, while end-of-run heaters have only one cable.

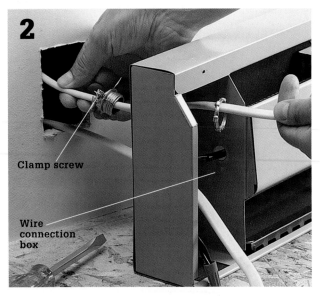

2

Clamp screw

Wire connection box

Remove the cover on the wire connection box. Open a knockout for each cable that will enter the box, then feed the cables through the cable clamps and into the wire connection box. Attach the clamps to the wire connection box and tighten the clamp screws until the cables are gripped firmly.

3

Anchor heater against wall about 1" off the floor by driving flathead screws through back of housing and into studs. Strip away cable sheathing so at least ½" of sheathing extends into the heater. Strip ¾" of insulation from each wire using a combination tool.

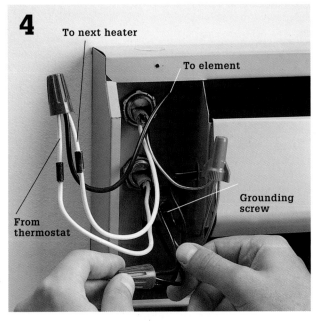

4

To next heater

To element

From thermostat

Grounding screw

Make connections to the heating element if the power wires are coming from a thermostat or another heater controlled by a thermostat. Connect the white circuit wires to one of the wire leads on the heater. Tag white wires with black tape to indicate they are hot. Connect the black circuit wires to the other wire lead. Connect a grounding pigtail to the green grounding screw in the box, then join all grounding wires with a wire connector. Reattach cover.

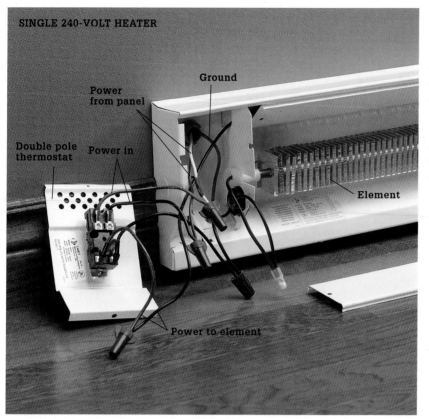

SINGLE 240-VOLT HEATER

Ground

Power from panel

Double pole thermostat

Power in

Element

Power to element

One heater with end-cap thermostat. Run both power leads (black plus tagged neutral) into the connection box at either end of the heater. If installing a single-pole thermostat, connect one power lead to one thermostat wire and connect the other thermostat wire to one of the heater leads. Connect the other hot LINE wire to the other heater lead. If you are installing a double-pole thermostat, make connections with both legs of the power supply.

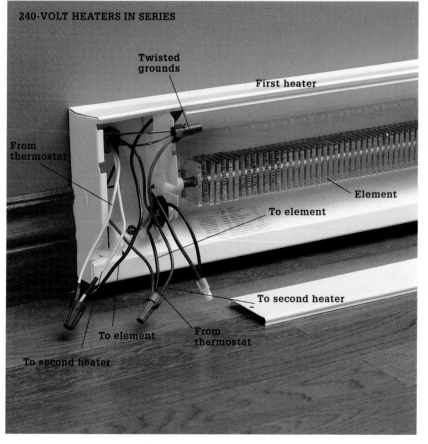

240-VOLT HEATERS IN SERIES

Twisted grounds

First heater

From thermostat

Element

To element

To second heater

To element

From thermostat

To second heater

Multiple heaters. At the first heater, join both hot wires from the thermostat to the wires leading to the second heater in line. Be sure to tag all white neutrals hot. Twist copper ground wires together and pigtail them to the grounding screw in the baseboard heater junction box. This parallel wiring configuration ensures that power flow will not be interrupted to the downstream heaters if an upstream heater fails.

Upgrading Ventilation

In basements it is especially important that air be kept moving constantly. High humidity levels combined with still or stagnant air leads to buildup of mold and mildew. If your basement rooms are part of a whole house, forced-air heating and cooling system, the natural air movement created when the system is operating will provide adequate air movement so no additional ventilation provisions need to be made (except in basement bathrooms, where a vent fan with an exterior exhaust is required).

If your basement has an independent heating system (such as electric baseboard heaters) and does not have air conditioning, add a ceiling-mounted vent fan in every room. If the rooms regularly have a musty odor, a vent fan is a good idea regardless of what type of heating and cooling plant you have.

Note: High-efficiency furnaces and water heaters have very specific requirements for fresh air intake supply. It is important that you consult with the furnace installer or your local plumbing inspector if you are making alterations to the airflow patterns in your basement.

Wiring a Vent Fan ▸

This layout lets you place two switches controlled by the same 120-volt circuit in one double-gang electrical box. A single-feed cable provides power to both switches. A standard switch controls the light fixture and a time-delay switch controls the vent fan.

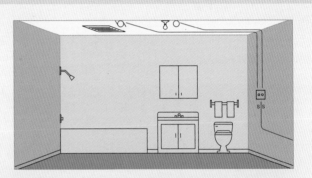

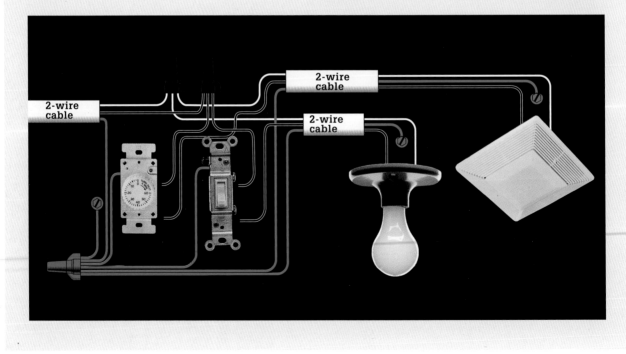

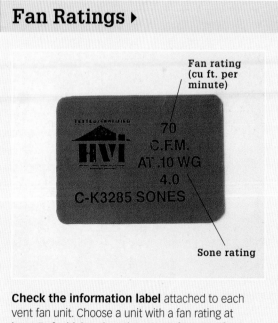

A vent fan is required in any basement bathroom. Hooking up the fan unit is easy, but running the exhaust ductwork can be tricky since it is normally vented outdoors through the rim joist.

Clothes dryers must be vented outdoors through ductwork. You may not vent them elsewhere in the basement.

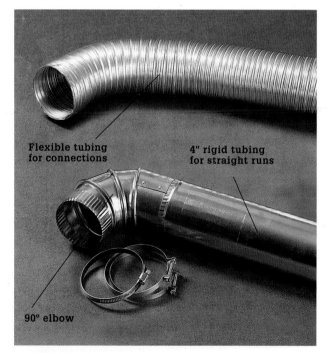

Flexible tubing
for connections

4" rigid tubing
for straight runs

90° elbow

Flexible metal tubing may be used to make the exhaust connection at the dryer, but the rest of the ductwork should be 4" rigid metal tubing.

Fan Ratings ▸

Fan rating
(cu ft. per
minute)

TESTED/CERTIFIED

HVI

70
C.F.M.
AT .10 WG
4.0
C-K3285 SONES

Sone rating

Check the information label attached to each vent fan unit. Choose a unit with a fan rating at least 5 cfm higher than the square footage of your bathroom. The sone rating refers to quietness rated on a scale of 1 to 7; quieter is lower.

How to Install Ventilation Ducts

To plan your vent pipe route (it can be no longer than 25 ft. in most places), start outdoors by establishing the best location for the vent hood. The ideal location is concealed from sight and kept away from windows. In most cases, it is easiest to run the pipe through the rim joist of your house, but you may have to cut through a masonry foundation wall. Choose a spot and mark it with tape.

Look for a distinguishing point in the house structure that you can locate precisely on the interior side. A window, sillcock, or another penetration in the rim joist is perfect. Measure the distance from the point to the marked area where you want to install the vent hood.

On the interior side of the wall, generally in the basement, measure from the structural object you identified to see if the potential location for the rim joist entry is clear and accessible. Also check to see if you can make a relatively clean run to the vent fan, with minimal turns and minimal cutting of floor joists. Finding the best spot will probably take some trial and error and compromising.

Outline a hole that's slightly larger in diameter than the vent fitting that will go through the wall. Drill through the hole center into the rim joist using a bit that's long enough to penetrate the exterior. Drill until the bit breaks through into the light of day. *Note: Holes must be at least 2" from either edge of the joist and their diameter cannot be more than ⅓ of the joist width.*

Cut the siding using the drill hole in the siding as a centerpoint, draw the outline for the cutout on the siding of your house. Cut out with a reciprocating saw and remodeler's blade.

Test the fit of the vent pipe assembly after you remove the cutout section of siding and joist material. Widen the hole if necessary. Once the assembly fits, slide the vent hood and pipe assembly into the hole so the vent hood flange fits as snugly against the siding as possible.

7

Attach the vent hood to the siding by driving screws at the corners.

8

Apply exterior-rated caulk around the perimeter of the vent hood to make a watertight seal. Snap on the protective cage, if provided, to keep small animals out.

9

Loosely pack fiberglass insulation between the vent duct and the edges of the opening you cut. Or, fill the gaps with minimal expanding spray foam insulation.

10

Run rigid metal ductwork from the vent hood to the fan. If you can, plan the route so you're installing the ductwork in the floor joist cavity. This will leave more headroom and lessen the chance of damaging the material.

11

Install an elbow at the end of the horizontal duct so it connects to the vent hood. Then add ductwork to connect the other side of the elbow to the vent.

Adding Electrical Circuits

Finishing a basement almost always requires that you add electrical circuits to service the new space. To determine your electrical needs, think about the finished space and the types of fixtures you plan to include. Also, consult the local building department to make sure your plans comply with local codes. The following are some of the basic electrical elements to consider.

The National Electrical Code (NEC) requires receptacles to be spaced no more than 12 ft. apart, but for convenience you can space them as close as 6 ft. apart. You may need some non-standard receptacles, such as a GFCI (for bathrooms and wet areas), a 20-amp or 240-volt receptacle (for large appliances), and an isolated-ground receptacle (for a computer). Also consider the placement of furniture in the finished room; avoid placing receptacles or baseboard heaters where they may be blocked by furniture.

Lighting is an important consideration for every room, particularly rooms with limited sources of ambient light. Most codes require that each room have at least one switch-controlled light fixture, with the switch placed near the room's entrance. Stairways

must have lighting that illuminates each step, and the fixture must be controlled by three-way switches at the top and bottom landings. Hallways and closets also need switch-controlled lights. In addition to meeting code requirements, your lighting plan should include different types of lighting to provide versatility for everyday tasks as well as visual warmth. This is especially true in basements, which generally need more artificial light than upper floors. It helps to use plenty of indirect lighting to eliminate shadows and provide ambient background light.

Your basement room may need additional wiring to supply auxiliary HVAC equipment, such as a baseboard heater. If you'll be installing an electric radiant heating system for supplemental heat, find out what type of circuit wiring the system requires.

One way to avoid long wiring runs and crowding of the main service panel is to install a circuit breaker subpanel in or near the finished space. A subpanel gets its power supply from a single cable leading from the main panel. With adequate amperage, a subpanel can serve all of the circuits necessary for the finished space—all from a convenient location.

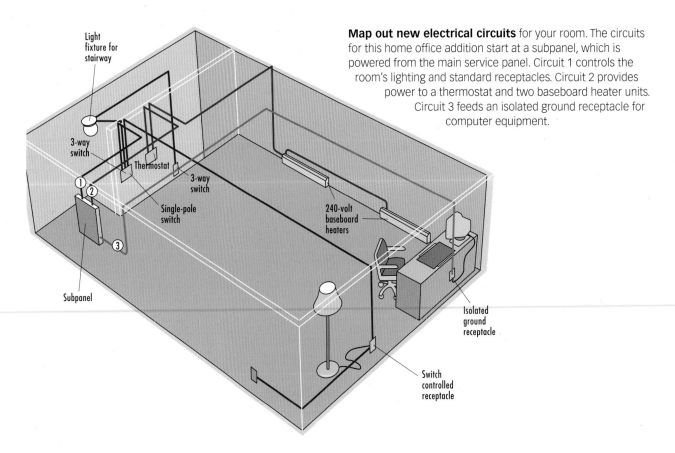

Map out new electrical circuits for your room. The circuits for this home office addition start at a subpanel, which is powered from the main service panel. Circuit 1 controls the room's lighting and standard receptacles. Circuit 2 provides power to a thermostat and two baseboard heater units. Circuit 3 feeds an isolated ground receptacle for computer equipment.

Light fixture for stairway

3-way switch

Thermostat

3-way switch

Single-pole switch

240-volt baseboard heaters

Subpanel

Isolated ground receptacle

Switch controlled receptacle

Planning Wiring Circuits

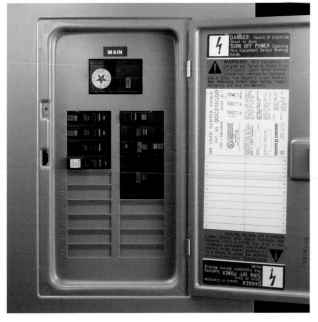

Examine your main service. The amp rating of the electrical service and the size of the circuit breaker panel will help you determine if a service upgrade is needed.

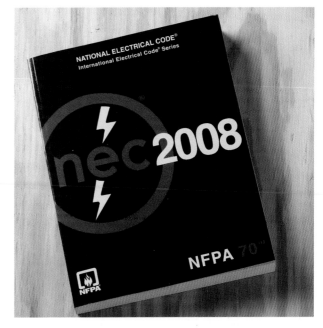

Learn about codes. The (NEC) and local electrical codes and building codes, provide guidelines for determining how much power and how many circuits your home needs. Your local electrical inspector can tell you which regulations apply to your job.

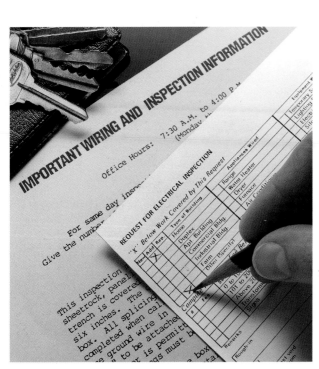

Prepare for inspections. Remember that your work must be reviewed by your local electrical inspector. When planning your wiring project, always follow the inspector's guidelines for quality workmanship.

Evaluate electrical loads. New circuits put an added load on your electrical service. Make sure that the total load of the existing wiring and the planned new circuits does not exceed the main service capacity.

Your Main Service Panel

Every home has a main service panel that distributes electrical current to the individual circuits. The main service panel is usually found in the basement, garage, or utility area, and can be identified by its metal casing. Before making any repair to your electrical system, you must shut off power to the correct circuit at the main service panel. The service panel should be indexed so circuits can be identified easily.

Service panels vary in appearance, depending on the age of the system. Very old wiring may operate on 30-amp service that has only two circuits. New homes can have 200-amp service with 30 or more circuits. Find the size of the service by reading the amperage rating printed on the main fuse block or main circuit breaker.

Regardless of age, all service panels have fuses or circuit breakers (page 59) that control each circuit and protect them from overloads. In general, older service panels use fuses, while newer service panels use circuit breakers.

In addition to the main service panel, your electrical system may have a subpanel that controls some of the circuits in the home. A subpanel has its own circuit breakers or fuses and is installed to control circuits that have been added to an existing wiring system.

The subpanel resembles the main service panel but is usually smaller. It may be located near the main panel, or it may be found near the areas served by the new circuits. Garages and basements that have been updated often have their own subpanels. If your home has a subpanel, make sure that its circuits are indexed correctly.

When handling fuses or circuit breakers, make sure the area around the service panel is dry. Never remove the protective cover on the service panel. After turning off a circuit to make electrical repairs, remember to always test the circuit for power before touching any wires.

The main service panel is the heart of your wiring system. As our demand for household energy has increased, the panels have also grown in capacity. Today, a 200-amp panel is considered the minimum for new construction.

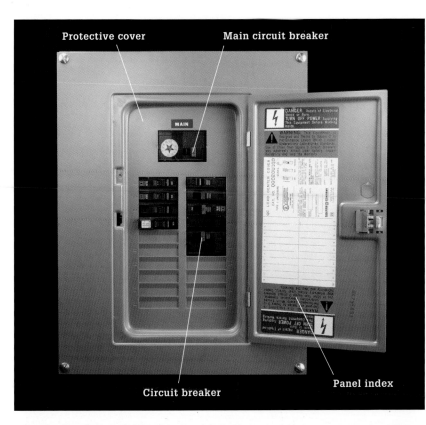

Protective cover   Main circuit breaker

MAIN

Circuit breaker   Panel index

A circuit breaker panel providing 100 amps or more of power is common in wiring systems installed during the 1960s and later. A circuit breaker panel is housed in a gray metal cabinet that contains two rows of individual circuit breakers. The size of the service can be identified by reading the amperage rating of the main circuit breaker, which is located at the top or bottom of the main service panel.

A 100-amp service panel is now the minimum standard for all new housing. It is considered adequate for a medium-sized house with no more than three major electrical appliances. However, larger houses with more electrical appliances require a service panel that provides 150 amps or more; 200 amps are becoming the standard.

To shut off power to individual circuits in a circuit breaker panel, flip the lever on the appropriate circuit breaker to the OFF position. To shut off the power to the entire house, turn the main circuit breaker to the OFF position.

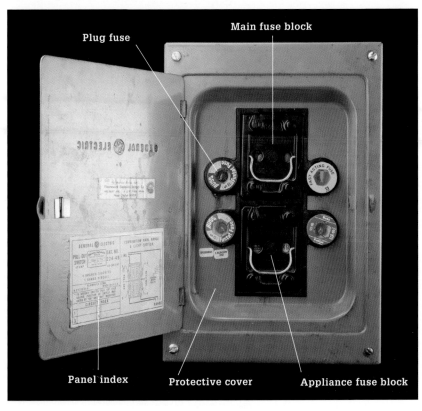

Plug fuse   Main fuse block

Panel index   Protective cover   Appliance fuse block

A 60-amp fuse panel is often found in wiring systems installed between 1950 and 1965. It is usually housed in a gray metal cabinet that contains four individual plug fuses, plus one or two pull-out fuse blocks that hold cartridge fuses. This type of panel is regarded as adequate for a small, 1,100-sq ft. house that has no more than one 240-volt appliance. Many homeowners update 60-amp service to 100 amps or more so that additional lighting and appliance circuits can be added to the system. Home loan programs also may require that 60-amp service be updated before a home can qualify for financing.

To shut off power to a circuit, carefully unscrew the plug fuse, touching only its insulated rim. To shut off power to the entire house, hold the handle of the main fuse block and pull sharply to remove it. Major appliance circuits are controlled with another cartridge fuse block. Shut off the appliance circuit by pulling out this fuse block.

Connecting Breakers for New Circuits

The last step in a wiring project is connecting circuits at the breaker panel. After this is done, the work is ready for the final inspection.

Circuits are connected at the main breaker panel if it has enough open slots, or at a circuit breaker subpanel. When working at a subpanel, make sure the feeder breaker at the main panel has been turned off, and test for power (photo, right) before touching any parts in the subpanel.

Make sure the circuit breaker amperage does not exceed the ampacity of the circuit wires you are connecting to it. Also be aware that circuit breaker styles and installation techniques vary according to manufacturer. Use breakers designed for your type of panel.

Tools & Materials ▶

Screwdriver
Hammer
Pencil
Combination tool
Cable ripper

Circuit tester
Pliers
Cable clamps
Single- and double-pole
   circuit breakers

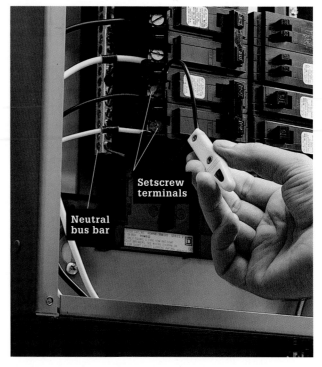

Test for current before touching any parts inside a circuit breaker panel. With the main breaker turned off but all other breakers turned on, touch one probe of a neon tester to the neutral bus bar, and touch the other probe to each setscrew on one of the double-pole breakers (not the main breaker). If tester does not light for either setscrew, it is safe to work in the panel.

How to Connect Circuit Breakers

Remove the panel cover plate after you shut off the main circuit breaker in the main circuit breaker panel. (If you are working in a subpanel, shut off the feeder breaker in the main panel.) Take care not to touch the parts inside the panel. Test for power.

Open a knockout in the side of the circuit breaker panel using a screwdriver and hammer. Attach a cable clamp to the knockout.

Hold cable across the front of the panel near the knockout, and mark sheathing about ½" inside the edge of the panel. Strip the cable from marked line to end using a cable ripper. (There should be 18 to 24" of excess cable.) Insert the cable through the clamp and into the service panel, then tighten the clamp.

Bend the bare copper grounding wire around the inside edge of the panel to an open setscrew terminal on the grounding bus bar. Insert the wire into the opening on the bus bar, and tighten the setscrew. Fold excess wire around the inside edge of the panel.

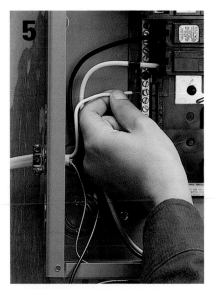

Bend the white circuit wire for 120-volt circuits around the outside of the panel to an open setscrew terminal on the neutral bus bar. Clip away excess wire, then strip ½" of insulation from the wire using a combination tool. Insert the wire into the terminal opening, and tighten the setscrew.

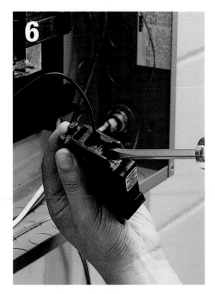

Strip ½" of insulation from the end of the black circuit wire. Insert the wire into the setscrew terminal on a new single-pole circuit breaker, and tighten the setscrew.

Slide one end of the circuit breaker onto the guide hook, then press it firmly against the bus bar until it snaps into place. (Breaker installation may vary depending on the manufacturer.) Fold excess black wire around the inside edge of the panel.

120/240-volt circuits (top): Connect red and black wires to a double-pole breaker. Connect white wire to the neutral bus bar, and grounding wire to the grounding bus bar. For 240-volt circuits (bottom), attach white and black wires to the double-pole breaker, tagging white wire with black tape. There is no neutral bus bar connection on this circuit.

Remove the appropriate breaker knockout on the panel cover plate to make room for the new circuit breaker. A single-pole breaker requires one knockout, while a double-pole breaker requires two knockouts. Reattach the cover plate, and label the new circuit on the panel index.

How to Run New Circuit Cable

Drill ⅝" holes in framing members for the cable runs. This is done easily with a right-angle drill, available at rental centers. Holes should be set back at least 1¼" from the front face of the framing members.

Where cables will turn corners, drill intersecting holes in adjoining faces of studs. Measure and cut all cables, allowing 2 ft. extra at ends entering the breaker panel and 1 ft. for ends entering the electrical box.

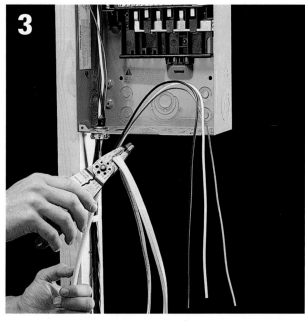

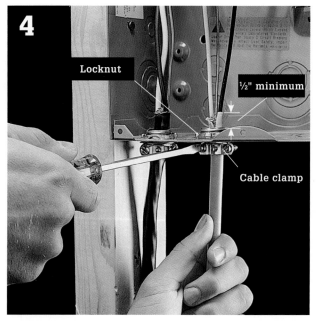

Shut off power to circuit breaker panel. Use a cable ripper to strip cable, leaving at least ¼" of sheathing to enter the circuit breaker panel. Clip away the excess sheathing.

Open a knockout in the circuit breaker panel using a hammer and screwdriver. Insert a cable clamp into the knockout, and secure it with a locknut. Insert the cable through the clamp so that at least ½" of sheathing extends inside the circuit breaker panel. Tighten the mounting screws on the clamp so the cable is gripped securely but not so tightly that the sheathing is crushed.

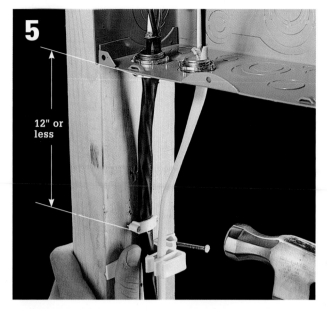

Anchor the cable to the center of a framing member within 12" of the circuit breaker panel using a cable staple. Stack-It® staples work well where two or more cables must be anchored to the same side of a stud. Run the cable to the first electrical box. Where the cable runs along the sides of framing members, anchor it with cable staples no more than 4 ft. apart.

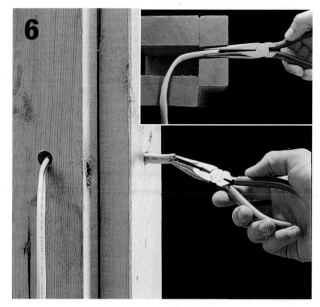

At corners, form a slight L-shaped bend in the end of the cable and insert it into one hole. Retrieve the cable through the other hole using needlenose pliers (inset).

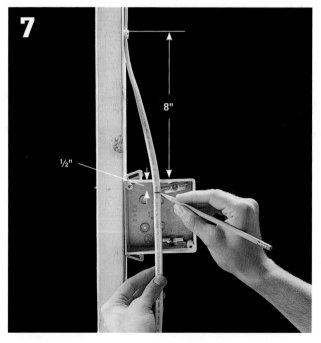

Staple the cable to a framing member 8" from the box. Hold the cable taut against the front of the box, and mark a point on the sheathing ½" past the box edge. Remove sheathing from the marked line to the end using a cable ripper, and clip away excess sheathing with a combination tool. Insert the cable through the knockout in the box.

Variation: Different types of boxes have different clamping devices. Make sure cable sheathing extends ½" past the edge of the clamp to ensure that the cable is secure and that the wire won't be damaged by the edges of the clamp.

(continued)

8

Clip back each wire as each cable is installed in a box, so that 8" of workable wire extends past the front edge of the box.

9

Strip ¾" of insulation from each circuit wire in the box using a combination tool. Take care not to nick the copper.

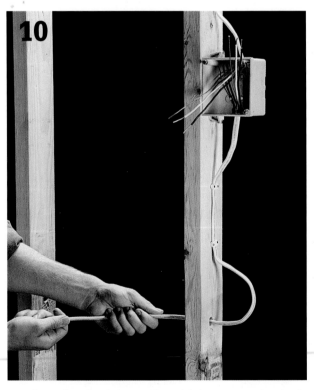

10

Continue the circuit by running cable between each pair of electrical boxes, leaving an extra 1 foot of cable at each end.

11

At metal boxes and recessed fixtures, open knockouts, and attach cables with cable clamps. From inside fixture, strip away all but ¼" of sheathing. Clip back wires so there is 8" of workable length, then strip ¾" of insulation from each wire.

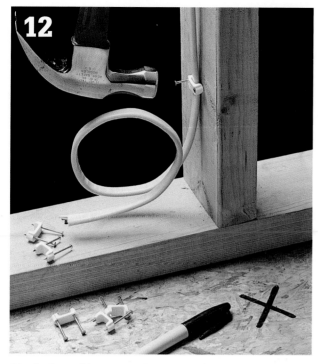

Staple the cable to a stud near the fixture location for a surface-mounted fixture like a baseboard heater or fluorescent light fixture. Leave plenty of excess cable. Mark the floor so the cable will be easy to find after the walls are finished.

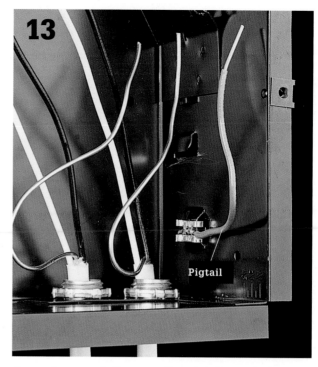

Connect one end of a grounding pigtail at each recessed fixture and metal electrical box, to the metal frame using a grounding clip attached to the frame (shown above) or a green grounding screw.

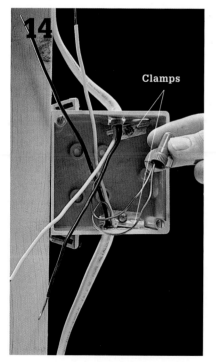

Join grounding wires together with a wire connector at each electrical box and recessed fixture. If the box has internal clamps, tighten the clamps over the cables.

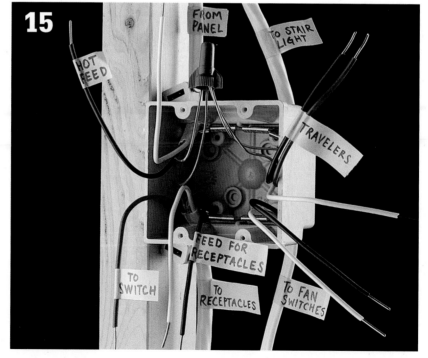

Label the cables entering each box to indicate their destinations. In boxes with complex wiring configurations, also tag the individual wires to make final hookups easier. After all the cables are installed, your rough-in work is ready to be reviewed by the electrical inspector.

Floors

Not every floor covering is well suited for basement floors, but there are enough good options to afford real choices. If you do extra preparation work, you may be able to install some flooring types that are typically not used in basements.

Flooring that can be installed with relatively little floor preparation includes ceramic tile and wood laminate strips. In most cases, the thinset mortar that serves as the bed for floor tiles can be applied directly to the concrete, and the laminate strips can be laid on top of a thin foam underlayment pad that's rolled out onto the concrete.

Other flooring types that work well in basements include sheet vinyl, vinyl tile, and some types of carpeting. All of these are best installed with an underlayment layer and a subfloor. The subfloor can be installed on wood sleepers to raise it off the concrete, or you can select subfloor panels with a built-in isolation layer.

The primary goal when choosing flooring for a basement is to select a product that does not readily absorb water and is easy to clean.

In this chapter:

- Preparing Basement Floors
- Creating Decorative Concrete Finishes
- Installing Radiant Floors
- Laying Tile Floors
- Installing Laminate Plank Floors
- Laying Resilient Tile Floors
- Installing Rubber Roll Floors
- Laying Carpet

Preparing Basement Floors

Preparing a concrete floor for carpet, laminate, vinyl, or wood flooring has been simplified by the introduction of new subfloor products that have built-in vapor barriers and cleats that create a slight air gap between the subfloor and the concrete slab. This system allows air to circulate, protecting the finished flooring from any slab moisture. The new dry-floor subfloor systems are less than one inch thick and are very easy to install. There are several types of these dry-floor systems available, but the one most readily available and easiest to use is a product sold in 2 × 2 feet tongue-and-groove squares.

Although subfloor panels can be adjusted for slight irregularities in the concrete slab, they can't overcome problems with a floor that is badly cracked and heaved. Nor is the built-in air gap beneath the system a solution to a basement that has serious water problems. A badly heaved slab will need to be leveled with a cement-based leveling compound, and serious water problems will need to be rectified before you consider creating finished living space in a basement.

Allow the subfloor panel squares to acclimate in the basement for at least 24 hours with the plastic surfaces facing down before installing them. In humid summer months, the squares—as well as the finished wood flooring product, if that's what you'll be installing—should be allowed to acclimate for a full two weeks before installation.

The old way of installing subfloor (plywood over 2 × 4 sleepers) does make a sturdy floor and has the advantage of not requiring any special products—you can do it with materials found at any building center.

Instead of a subfloor and plywood underlayment, some flooring requires an isolation layer to separate it from the concrete basement floor. These are most often installed with ceramic floors.

If your concrete basement floor has cracks, holes, or other imperfections, address them before installing flooring.

Shown cutaway for clarity

Wood laminate flooring

Dry-floor subfloor square

Underlayment

Basement slab

Concrete basement floors have a high utility value, but whenever possible you'll want to cover them to improve livability in your new basement rooms. Some floor coverings can be installed directly over the concrete, but in most cases you should lay subfloor panels and underlayment before installing the floor covering. A system like the one above is ideal for basements because it can be removed readily: the laminate strip flooring snaps together and apart; the underlayment is unbonded and can be rolled up; and the subfloor panels also are snap-together for easy removal and re-laying.

Apply Floor Leveler ▸

Use floor leveler mix or a mortar mixture to fill in small dips in the concrete floor.

Leveling Basement Floors

Level line

Laser level

Test the floor to see how level it is. Use a laser level to project a level line on all walls. Mark the line and then measure down to the floor. Compare measurements to determine if floor is level. If you are installing a subfloor you can correct the unevenness by shimming under low areas. But if the floor height varies by more than an inch or two (not uncommon), you should pour floor leveler compound in the low areas. In more extreme examples you'll need to resurface the entire floor.

Break up and remove very high areas or eruptions, and patch the area with concrete that is leveled with the surrounding surfaces. Use a rental jack hammer to break up the concrete. A hand maul and cold chisel also may be used if the area is not too large: most concrete basement floors are only 3 to 4" thick.

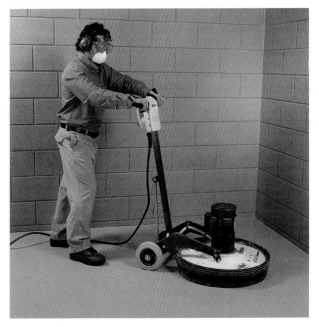

Grind down high spots if they are small and far apart. A rented concrete grinder makes quick work of the job. Even larger areas can be ground down, if your ceiling height is already limited (less than 7 ft.).

How to Repair Floor Cracks

Prepare the crack for the repair materials by knocking away any loose or deteriorating material and beveling the edges down and outward with a cold chisel. Sweep or vacuum the debris and thoroughly dampen the repair area. Do not allow any water to pool, however.

Mix the repair product to fill the crack according to the manufacturer's instructions. Here, a fast-setting cement repair product with acrylic fortifier is being used. Trowel the product into the crack, overfilling slightly. With the edge of the trowel, trim the excess material and feather it so it is smooth and the texture matches the surrounding surface.

How to patch a small hole

Cut out around the damaged area with a masonry-grinding disc mounted on a portable drill (or use a hammer and stone chisel). The cuts should bevel about 15° away from the center of the damaged area. Chisel out any loose concrete within the repair area. Always wear gloves and eye protection.

Dampen the repair area with clean water and then fill it with vinyl concrete patcher. Pack the material in with a trowel, allowing it to crown slightly above the surrounding surface. Then, feather the edges so the repair is smooth and flat. Protect the repair from foot traffic for at least one day and from vehicle traffic for three days.

How to Patch a Large Hole

Use a hammer and chisel or a heavy floor scraper to remove all material that is loose or shows any deterioration. Thoroughly clean the area with a hose and nozzle or a pressure washer.

OPTION: Make beveled cuts around the perimeter of the repair area with a circular saw and masonry-cutting blade. The bevels should slant down and away from the damage to create a "key" for the repair material.

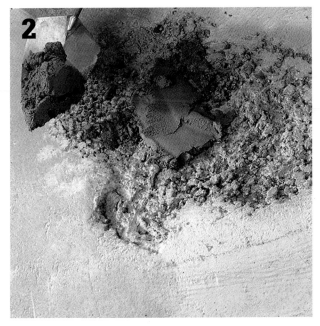

Mix concrete patching compound according to the manufacturer's instructions, and then trowel it neatly into the damage area, which should be dampened before the patching material is placed. Overfill the damage area slightly.

Smooth and feather the repair with a steel trowel so it is even with the surrounding concrete surface. Finish the surface of the repair material to blend with the existing surface. For example, use a whisk broom to recreate a broomed finish. Protect the repair from foot traffic for at least one day and from vehicle traffic for three days.

Resurfacing a Concrete Floor

Badly degraded concrete basement floors can be restored by applying a topcoat of floor resurfacer. This cement-based product is designed to be poured on as a thick liquid so it can use gravity to find and fill in the low areas. After the resurfacer has set up, you will have a surface that's flat and smooth enough for installing just about any floorcovering you choose, including padded carpet and floating floors with underlayment pads.

Concrete resurfacer typically should not be applied in layers thicker than one-half inch. If your floor has low areas greater than this, fill them with sand-mix concrete first to get the low spots close to level, and then top with resurfacer over the whole floor.

Tools & Materials ▸

Pressure washer
Steel concrete
 finishing trowel
Long-handled
 squeegee
5-gallon bucket

½" drill with paddle
 mixer
Duct tape or backer rod
Stiff-bristle brush
Concrete resurfacer

BEFORE   AFTER

Concrete resurfacer offers an easy, inexpensive solution for renewing concrete surfaces in basements.

How to Resurface a Concrete Floor

1

Thoroughly clean the entire project area. If necessary, remove all oil and greasy or waxy residue using a concrete cleaner and scrub brush. Water beading on the surface indicates residue that could prevent proper adhesion with the resurfacer; clean these areas again as needed.

2

Wash the concrete with a pressure washer. Hold the fan-spray tip about 3" from the surface or as recommended by the washer manufacturer. Remove standing water.

3

Fill sizeable pits and spalled areas using a small batch of concrete resurfacer—mix about 5 pints of water per 40-lb. bag of resurfacer for a trowelable consistency. Repair cracks as shown on page 70. Smooth the repairs level with the surrounding surface, and let them harden.

4

Section off the slab on a large project into areas no larger than 100 sq. ft. It's easiest to delineate sections along existing control joints. On all projects, cover or seal off all control joints with duct tape, foam backer rod, or weatherstripping to prevent resurfacer from spilling into the joints.

5

Mix the desired quantity of concrete resurfacer with water, following the mixing instructions. Work the mix with a ½" drill and a mixing paddle for 5 minutes to achieve a smooth, pourable consistency. If necessary, add water sparingly until the mix will pour easily and spread well with a squeegee.

6

Saturate the work area with water, then use a squeegee to remove any standing water. Pour the mix of concrete resurfacer onto the center of the repair area or first repair section.

7

Spread the resurfacer with the squeegee, using a scrubbing motion to make sure all depressions are filled. Then spread it into a smooth, consistent layer. If desired, broom the surface for a nonslip finish. You can also tool the slab edges with a concrete edger within 20 minutes of application. Let the resurfacer cure.

How to Install Isolation Membrane

Isolation membrane is used to protect ceramic tile installations from movement that may occur on cracked concrete floors. This product is used primarily for covering individual cracks, but it can be used over an entire floor. Isolation membrane is also available in a liquid form that can be poured over the project area.

Thoroughly clean the subfloor, then apply thin-set mortar with a ⅛" notched trowel. Start spreading the mortar along the floor in a section as wide as the membrane and 8 to 10 ft. long. *Note: For some membranes, you must use a bonding material other than mortar. Read and follow manufacturer's directions.*

Roll out the membrane over the mortar. Cut the membrane to fit tightly against the walls using a straightedge and utility knife.

Starting in the center of the membrane, use a heavy floor roller to smooth·out the surface toward the edges. This frees trapped air and presses out excess bonding material.

Repeat steps 1 through 3, cutting the membrane as necessary at the walls and obstacles, until the floor is completely covered with membrane. Do not overlap the seams, but make sure they're tight. Allow the mortar to set for two days before installing the tile.

Subfloor Preparation by Flooring Type

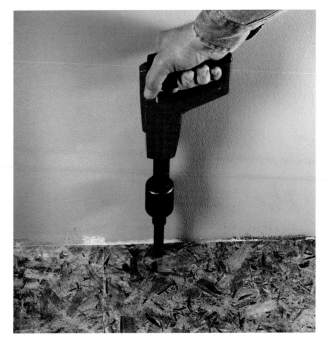

Dry-floor panels are needed if carpeting will be installed. Anchor the panels to the floor around the perimeter of the room and at the center of the room using concrete masonry anchors. Use a powder-actuated nailer to drive 2" nails through the panels and into the concrete slab.

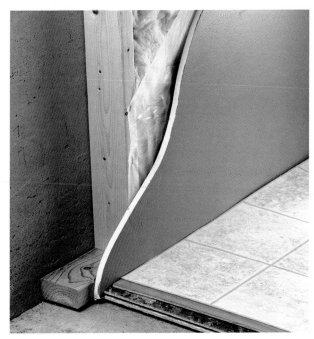

Resilient flooring for engineered wood flooring, install ¼" plywood underlayment over the dry-floor panels, using ½" screws or nails, which won't penetrate the moisture barrier on the underside of the panels. Don't glue the plywood to the subfloor panels, and never glue vinyl flooring directly to the subfloor panels.

For ceramic tile, install ½" cementboard over the subfloor panels, and attach it using ¾" screws. You may also set tiles into a mortar bed that's spread directly onto the concrete if the floor is in good shape. Another option to the construction shown above is to install an isolation membrane instead of a subfloor so cracks do not telegraph (see previous page).

Transition strips ▸

Transition strip

In some cases you'll need to install more than one type of flooring, which can cause you to have different finished floor heights. In these situations, install transition strips or reducers (sold at flooring retailers) to bridge the changes in floor height.

How to Install Interlocking Subfloor Panels

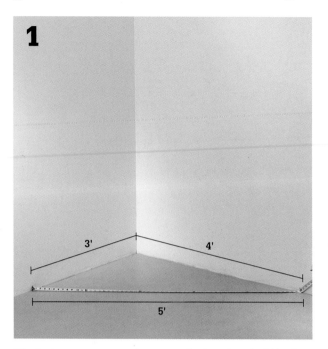

1

Start at one corner, and measure the length and width of the room from that starting point. Calculate the number of panels you will need to cover the space in both directions. If the starting corner is not square, trim the first row to create a straight starting line.

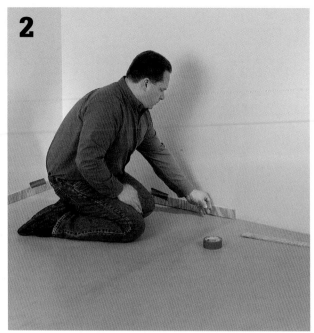

2

Create an expansion gap around the edges. Place ¼" spacers at all walls, doors, and other large obstacles. To make your own spacers, cut sheets of ¼" plywood to the thickness of the panels and hold them in place temporarily with adhesive tape.

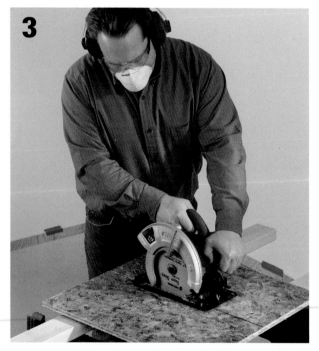

3

Dry-lay a row of panels across the room. If the last row will be less than 6" wide, balance it by trimming the first panel or the starting row, if necessary, to account for the row end pieces.

4

Starting in the corner, lay the first panel with the grooved side against the ¼" spacers. Slide the next panel into place and press-fit the groove of the second panel onto the tongue of the first. Check the edges against the wall.

5

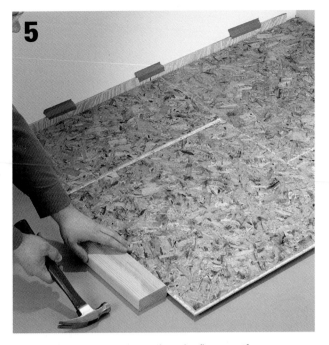

Repeat these steps to complete the first row. If necessary, tap the panels into place with a scrap piece of lumber and a rubber mallet or hammer—just be careful not to damage the tongue or groove edges.

6

Cut the last panel to fit snugly between the next-to-last panel and the ¼" spacer on the far wall. Install the last panel at an angle and tap it down. Starting with the second row, stagger the seams so that the panels interlock. Continue working from the starting point, checking after each row to be sure the panels are square and level.

7

When you reach the last row and last panel to complete your installation, you may have to cut the panel to fit. Measure for fit, allowing for the ¼" expansion gap from the wall. Cut the panel and fit it into place.

8

Remove the spacers from around the perimeter of the room when all the panels are in place and the finished floor is installed.

Tip ▶

If the room has a floor drain, building code requires that you cut a round patch in the panel that falls directly over the floor drain. This patch can be removed to allow access to the floor drain, should it ever be necessary.

How to Install Subfloor Sleepers

The Sleeper System ▶

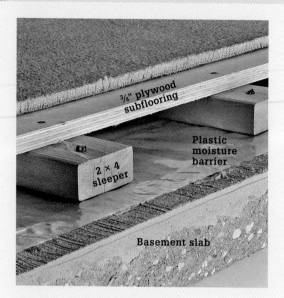

Sleepers are strips of lumber (2 x 4 or 1 x 4) that are laid over a moisture barrier on a concrete floor to serve as nailers for the subfloor and to isolate it from direct contact with the concrete floor.

1

Roll out strips of 6-mil polyethylene sheeting. Overlap strips by 6", then seal the seams with vapor barrier, tape, or packing tape. Temporarily tape the edges along the walls. Be careful not to damage the sheeting.

2

Lay out pressure-treated 2 x 4s along the perimeter of the room. Position the boards ½" in from all walls (inset). *Note: Before laying out the sleepers, determine where the partition walls will go. If a wall will fall between parallel sleepers, add an extra sleeper to support the planned wall.*

3

Install sleepers using a circular saw, cut the sleepers to fit between the perimeter boards leaving a ¼" gap at each end. Position the first sleeper so its center is 16" from the outside edge of the perimeter board. Lay out the remaining sleepers using 16"-on-center spacing.

Where necessary, use tapered cedar shims to compensate for dips and variations in the floor. Place a 4-ft. level across neighboring sleepers. Apply construction adhesive to two wood shims. Slide the shims under the board from opposite sides until the board is level with adjacent sleepers.

Fasten the perimeter boards and sleepers to the floor using a powder-actuated nailer or masonry screws. Drive a fastener through the center of each board at 16" intervals. Fastener heads should not protrude above the board's surface. Place a fastener at each shim location, making sure the fastener penetrates both shims.

Establish a control line for the first row of plywood sheets by measuring 49" from the wall and marking the outside sleeper at each end of the room. Snap a chalk line across the sleepers at the marks. Run a ¼"-wide bead of adhesive along the first six sleepers, stopping just short of the control line.

Position the first sheet of ¾" plywood subfloor so the end is ½" away from the wall and the grooved edge is flush with the control line. Fasten the sheet to the sleepers using 2" wallboard screws. Drive a screw every 6" along the edges and every 8" in the field. Don't drive screws along the grooved edge until the next row of sheeting is in place.

Install the remaining sheets in the first row, maintaining an ⅛" gap between ends. Begin the second row with a half sheet (4 ft. long) so the end joints between rows are staggered. Fit the tongue of the half sheet into the groove of the adjoining sheet. If necessary, use a sledgehammer and wood block to help close the joint. After completing the second row, begin the third row with a full sheet. Alternate this pattern until the subfloor is complete.

Creating Decorative Concrete Finishes

Most people are accustomed to thinking of concrete primarily as a utilitarian substance, but it can also mimic a variety of flooring types and be a colorful and beautiful addition to your basement room.

Concrete is a hard and durable building material, but it is also porous—so it is susceptible to staining. Many stains can be removed with the proper cleaner, but sealing and painting prevents oil, grease, and other stains from penetrating the surface in the first place; and cleanup is a whole lot easier.

Even after degreasing a concrete floor, residual grease or oils can create serious adhesion problems for coatings of sealant or paint. To check to see whether your floor has been adequately cleaned, pour a glass of water on the concrete floor. If it is ready for sealing, the water will soak into the surface quickly and evenly. If the water beads, you may have to clean it again. Detergent used in combination with a steam cleaner can remove stubborn stains better than a cleaner alone.

There are four important reasons to seal your concrete floor: to protect the floor from dirt, oil, grease, chemicals, and stains; to dust-proof the surface; to protect the floor from abrasion and sunlight exposure; and to repel water and protect the floor from freeze-thaw damage.

Tools & Materials ▸

Acid-tolerant pump sprayer	Eye protection
Alkaline-base neutralizer	Garden hose with nozzle
Sealant	Paint roller frame Paint
Rubber Boots	Soft-woven roller cover
Rubber gloves	High-pressure washer
Roller tray	Paintbrush
Wet vacuum	Respirator
Acid-tolerant bucket	Stiff-bristle broom
	Extension handle

Etching and sealing a concrete floor that is in good condition yields a slick-looking surface that has a contemporary feel and is easy to maintain.

How to Seal Concrete Basement Floors

Clean and prepare the surface by first sweeping up all debris. Next, remove all surface muck: mud, wax, and grease. Finally, remove existing paints or coatings.

Saturate the surface with clean water. The surface needs to be wet before acid etching. Use this opportunity to check for any areas where water beads up. If water beads on the surface, contaminants still need to be cleaned off with a suitable cleaner or chemical stripper.

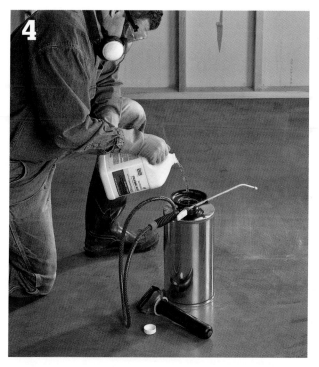

Test your acid-tolerant pump sprayer with water to make sure it releases a wide, even mist. Once you have the spray nozzle set, check the manufacturer's instructions for the etching solution and fill the pump sprayer (or sprinkling can) with the recommended amount of water.

Add the acid etching contents to the water in the acid-tolerant pump sprayer. Follow the directions (and mixing proportions) specified by the manufacturer. Use caution and wear safety equipment.

(continued)

Apply the acid solution. Using the sprinkling can or acid-tolerant pump spray unit, evenly apply the diluted acid solution over the concrete floor. Do not allow acid solution to dry at any time during the etching and cleaning process. Etch small areas at a time, 10 × 10 ft. or smaller. If there is a slope, begin on the low side of the slope and work upward.

Use a stiff-bristle broom or scrubber to work the acid solution into the concrete. Let the acid sit for 5 to 10 minutes, or as indicated by the manufacturer's directions. A mild foaming action indicates that the product is working. If no bubbling or fizzing occurs, it means there is still grease, oil, or a concrete treatment on the surface that is interfering. If this occurs, follow steps 7 to 12 and then clean again.

Once the fizzing has stopped, the acid has finished reacting with the alkaline concrete surface and formed pH-neutral salts. Neutralize any remaining acid with an alkaline-base solution. Put 1 gal. of water in a 5-gal. bucket and then stir in an alkaline-base neutralizer. Using a stiff-bristle broom, make sure the concrete surface is completely covered with the solution. Continue to sweep until the fizzing stops.

Use a garden hose with a pressure nozzle or, ideally, a pressure washer in conjunction with a stiff-bristle broom to thoroughly rinse the concrete surface. Rinse the surface two to three times. Reapply the acid (repeat steps 5, 6, 7, and 8).

If you have any leftover acid, you can make it safe for your septic system by mixing more alkaline solution in the 5-gal. bucket and carefully pouring the acid from the spray unit into the bucket until all of the fizzing stops.

Use a wet/dry vacuum to clean up the mess. Some sitting acids and cleaning solutions can harm local vegetation, damage your drainage system, and are just plain environmentally unfriendly. Check your local disposal regulations for proper disposal of the neutralized spent acid.

To check for residue, rub a dark cloth over a small area of concrete. If any white residue appears, continue the rinsing process. Check for residue again.

Let the concrete dry for at least 24 hours and sweep up dust, dirt, and particles leftover from the acid etching process. Your concrete should now have the consistency of 120-grit sandpaper and be able to accept concrete sealants.

How to Stain a Concrete Floor

Thoroughly clean the entire floor (see page 81). Use painter's tape and plastic sheeting to protect any areas that won't be stained, as well as surrounding walls and other surfaces. Test the spray of your garden sprayer using water: it should deliver a wide, even mist.

Dampen the floor with water using a garden sprayer. Mop up any pooled water, but make sure the entire floor is damp. Load sprayer with stain, and then apply the stain evenly in a circular motion until the concrete is saturated. Let the floor dry.

Remove the etching residue by soaking the floor with water and scrubbing vigorously with a stiff-bristled brush. As you work, clean up the liquid with a wet/dry vacuum. Dispose of the waste liquid safely, according to local regulations.

When the floor has dried completely (at least 18 to 24 hours), begin applying the sealer along the edges and in any hard-to-reach areas using a paintbrush.

Using a ⅜" nap roller, apply the sealer in 2 × 6-ft. sections, maintaining a wet edge to prevent lap marks. If the sealer rapidly sinks into the concrete, apply a second coat after 2 hours. Let the floor dry for 18 to 24 hours before allowing light foot traffic and 72 hours before heavy use.

How to Paint a Concrete Floor

If you expect to use more than one container of paint, open them all and mix them together for a uniform color. You do not need to thin a paint for use on a floor. One exception is if you use a sprayer that requires thinned paint.

Using a nylon brush, such as a 2½" sash brush, cut in the sides and corners with primer. This creates a sharp, clean edge. Start this way for the top coat as well.

Using a roller pad with the nap length recommended by the manufacturer, apply a primer coat to the surface. Start at the corner farthest away from the door, and back up as you work. Allow the primer to dry for at least 8 hours.

With a clean roller pad, apply the first top coat. Make the top coat even but not too thick, then let it dry for 24 hours. If you choose to add another top coat, work the roller in another direction to cover any thin spots. Let the final coat dry another day before you walk on it.

Installing Radiant Floors

Floor-warming systems require very little energy to run and are designed to heat ceramic tile floors only; they generally are not used as sole heat sources for rooms.

A typical floor-warming system consists of one or more thin mats containing electric resistance wires that heat up when energized like an electric blanket. The mats are installed beneath the tile and are hardwired to a 120-volt GFCI circuit. A thermostat controls the temperature, and a timer turns the system off automatically.

The system shown in this project includes two plastic mesh mats, each with its own power lead that is wired directly to the thermostat. Radiant mats may be installed over a plywood subfloor, but if you plan to install floor tile you should put down a base of cementboard first, and then install the mats on top of the cementboard.

A crucial part of installing this system is to use a multimeter to perform several resistance checks to make sure the heating wires have not been damaged during shipping or installation.

Electrical service required for a floor-warming system is based on size. A smaller system may connect to an existing GFCI circuit, but a larger one will need a dedicated circuit; follow the manufacturer's requirements.

To order a floor-warming system, contact the manufacturer or dealer (see Resources, page 252). In most cases, you can send them plans and they'll custom fit a system for your project area.

Tools & Materials ▸

Vacuum cleaner	Electric wire fault
Multimeter	indicator (optional)
Tape measure	Radiant floor mats
Scissors	12/2 NM cable
Router/rotary tool	Conduit
Marker	Wire connectors
Trowel	Thinset mortar
or rubber float	Thermostat with sensor
Notched trowel	Junction box(es)
Staple gun	Tile or stone floor
Hot glue gun	covering
Cable clamps	Spiral cutting tool

A radiant floor-warming system employs electric heating mats that are covered with floor tile to create a floor that's cozy underfoot.

Installation Tips ▸

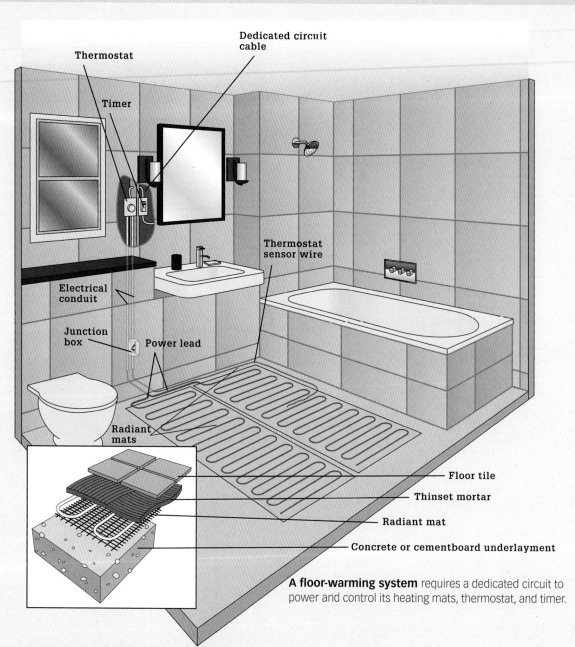

Thermostat

Dedicated circuit cable

Timer

Thermostat sensor wire

Electrical conduit

Junction box

Power lead

Radiant mats

Floor tile

Thinset mortar

Radiant mat

Concrete or cementboard underlayment

A floor-warming system requires a dedicated circuit to power and control its heating mats, thermostat, and timer.

- Each radiant mat must have a direct connection to the power lead from the thermostat, with the connection made in a junction box in the wall cavity. Do not install mats in series.
- Do not install radiant floor mats under shower areas.
- Do not overlap mats or let them touch.
- Do not cut heating wire or damage heating wire insulation.
- The distance between wires in adjoining mats should equal the distance between wire loops measured center to center.

Tips for Installing a Radiant Floor-Warming System

Floor-warming systems must be installed on a circuit with adequate amperage and a GFCI breaker. Smaller systems may tie into an existing circuit, but larger ones need a dedicated circuit. Follow local building and electrical codes that apply to your project.

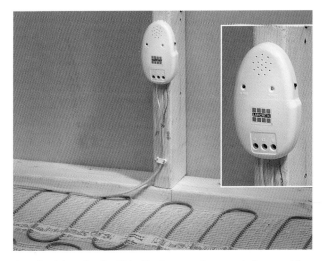

An electric wire fault indicator monitors each floor mat for continuity during the installation process. If there is a break in continuity (for example, if a wire is cut) an alarm sounds. If you choose not to use an installation tool to monitor the mat, test for continuity frequently using a multimeter.

How To Install a Radiant Floor-Warming System

Install an electrical box to house the thermostat and timer. In most cases, the box should be located 60" above floor level. Use a 4"-deep × 4"-wide double-gang box for the thermostat/timer control if your kit has an integral model. If your timer and thermostat are separate, install a separate single box for the timer.

Drill access holes in the sole plate for the power leads that are preattached to the mats (they should be over 10 ft. long). The leads should be connected to a supply wire from the thermostat in a junction box located in a wall near the floor and below the thermostat box. The access hole for each mat should be located directly beneath the knockout for that cable in the thermostat box. Drill through the sill plate vertically and horizontally so the holes meet in an L-shape.

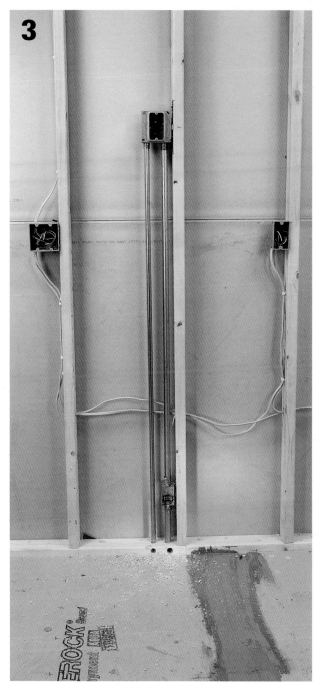

3

Run conduit from the electrical boxes to the sill plate. The line for the supply cable should be ¾" conduit. If you are installing multiple mats, the supply conduit should feed into a junction box about 6" above the sill plate and then continue into the ¾" hole you drilled for the supply leads. The sensor wire needs only ½" conduit that runs straight from the thermostat box via the thermostat. The mats should be powered by a dedicated 20-amp GFCI circuit of 12/2 NM cable run from your main service panel to the electrical box (this is for 120-volt mats—check your instruction manual for specific circuit recommendations).

4

Clean the floor surface thoroughly to get rid of any debris that could potentially damage the wire mats. A vacuum cleaner generally does a more effective job than a broom.

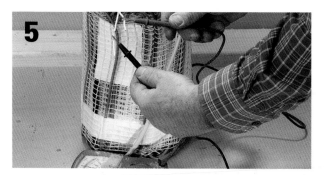

5

Test for resistance using a multimeter set to measure ohms. This is a test you should make frequently during the installation, along with checking for continuity. If the resistance is off by more than 10% from the theoretical resistance listing (see manufacturer's chart in installation instructions), contact a technical support operator for the kit manufacturer. For example, the theoretical resistance for the 1 × 50-ft. mat seen here is 19, so the ohms reading should be between 17 and 21.

6

Finalize your mat layout plan. Most radiant floor warming mat manufacturers will provide a layout plan for you at the time of purchase, or they will give you access to an online design tool so you can come up with your own plan. This is an important step to the success of your project, and the assistance is free.

(continued)

7

8

Unroll the radiant mat or mats and allow them to settle. Arrange the mat or mats according to the plan you created. It's okay to cut the plastic mesh so you can make curves or switchbacks, but do not cut the heating wire under any circumstances, even to shorten it.

Finalize the mat layout and then test the resistance again using a multimeter. Also check for continuity in several different spots. If there is a problem with any of the mats, you should identify it and correct it before proceeding with the mortar installation.

9

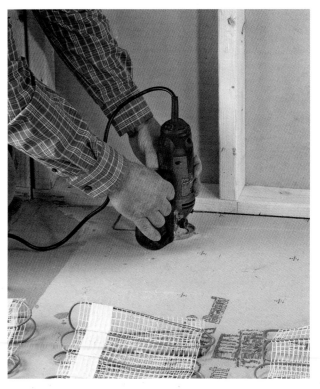

Run the thermostat sensor wire from the electrical box down the ½" conduit raceway and out the access hole in the sill plate. Select the best location for the thermostat sensor and mark the location on the flooring. Also mark the locations of the wires that connect to and lead from the sensor.

Variation: If your local codes require it, roll the mats out of the way and cut a channel for the sensor and the sensor wires into the floor or floor underlayment. For most floor materials, a spiral cutting tool does a quick and neat job of this task. Remove any debris.

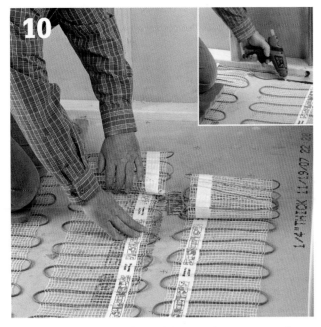

Bond the mats to the floor. If the mats in your system have adhesive strips, peel off the adhesive backing and roll out the mats in the correct position, pressing them against the floor to set the adhesive. If your mats have no adhesive, bind them with strips of double-sided carpet tape. The thermostat sensor and the power supply leads should be attached with hot glue (inset) and run up into their respective holes in the sill plate if you have not done this already. Test all mats for resistance and continuity.

Cover the floor installation areas with a layer of thinset mortar that is thick enough to fully encapsulate all the wires and mats (usually around ¼" in thickness). Check the wires for continuity and resistance regularly and stop working immediately if there is a drop in resistance or a failure of continuity. Allow the mortar to dry overnight.

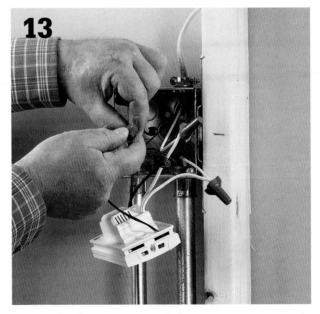

Connect the power supply leads from the mat or mats to the NM cable coming from the thermostat inside the junction box near the sill. Power must be turned off. The power leads should be cut so about 8" of wire feeds into the box. Be sure to use cable clamps to protect the wires.

Connect the sensor wire and the power supply lead (from the junction box) to the thermostat/timer according to the manufacturer's directions. Attach the device to the electrical box, restore power, and test the system to make sure it works. Once you are convinced that it is operating properly, install floor tiles and repair the wall surfaces.

Laying Tile Floors

Setting tile or flagstone on a concrete floor is a simple project. Its success depends on proper preparation of the concrete, a good layout, and attention to detail during the setting process. It's important to fill dips, cracks, and holes in the concrete with concrete patch or floor leveler before setting tile. If the surface is too uneven, the tile will crack when exposed to the pressure of foot traffic.

Choose tile or stone with enough texture to be a safe surface despite the moist conditions of a cellar. After you've chosen the tile or stone, ask your retailer about the appropriate mortar and grout for your application.

Before establishing reference lines for your project, think about where to start tiling. The goal is to continue working without having to step on previously laid tile.

Ceramic, porcelain, or stone tile is impervious to water and therefore makes an excellent flooring choice for basements. See page 75 for suggestions on floor preparation.

Tools & Materials ▸

2 × 4 with carpeting	Rubber gloves
Sponge	Concrete patching
Rubber mallet	compound
Paint roller	Floor leveler
Chalk line	compound
Framing square	Concrete sealer
¼" notched square	Grout sealer
trowel	Ceramic or stone tile
Wet saw	Thinset or other mortar
Needlenose pliers	Grout
Rubber grout float	Spacers
Trisodium phosphate	Paintbrush

Tool Tip ▸

Irregular cuts can be made by scoring with a handheld tile cutter (left photo), and then they can be finished with tile nippers (right photo).

How to Install Tile on a Basement Floor

Scrub the floor with a solution of trisodium phosphate (TSP) and water, let it dry completely, and then check the clean concrete for cracks, holes, and other damage. Fill cracks and holes with concrete patching compound (see pages 70 to 71). Apply concrete sealer to the clean, patched, and dry concrete. Use a paintbrush for the edges and the corners and a paint roller for the remaining areas.

Position a reference line (X) by measuring between opposite sides of the room and marking the center of each side. Snap a chalk line between these marks. Measure and mark the center point of the chalk line. From this point, use a framing square to establish a second line perpendicular to the first. Snap a second reference line (Y) across the room.

Test the layout by dry-setting one vertical and one horizontal row of tile all the way to the walls in both directions. If the layout results in uneven or awkward cuts at the edges, adjust the reference lines to produce a better layout.

Mix a batch of thinset mortar, following the manufacturer's directions. Spread mortar evenly against both reference lines of one quadrant. Use a ¼"-notched square trowel to create furrows in the mortar bed.

(continued)

Set the first tile in the corner of the quadrant where the reference lines intersect. When setting tiles that are 8" or larger, twist each tile slightly as you set it into position.

Using a soft rubber mallet, gently rap the central area of each tile a few times to set it evenly into the mortar. If the tile is not self-spacing, insert spacers at the corners of the tile.

Set tiles into the mortar along the reference lines. Cover a straight 2 × 4 with old carpeting and lay it across several tiles. Rap it with a mallet. Lay tile in the remaining area that has been covered with mortar. Work in small sections until you reach the walls. Cut tiles as needed using a wet saw (see photo right).

Apply mortar directly to the backs of smaller cut tiles, instead of the floor, using the notched edge of the trowel to furrow the mortar. Set the tiles.

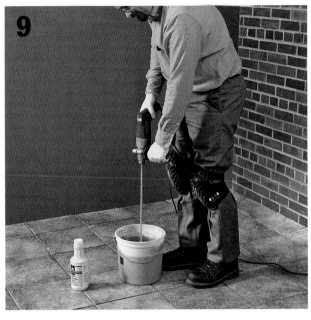

Choose a sanded grout color that complements your tile. Mix a small batch of grout following the manufacturer's directions. For unglazed or stone tile, add a release agent to keep the grout from bonding to the tile. *Tip: Dark grout doesn't show dirt but contrasts with lighter tile. Light grout is tough to keep looking clean. A midtone gray is often an excellent grout color.*

Starting in a corner, pour the grout over the tile. Spread the grout outward from the corner, pressing firmly on the grout float to completely fill the joints. Tilt the grout float at a 60° angle to the floor and use a figure-eight motion.

Use the grout float to remove excess grout from the surface of the tile. Wipe diagonally across the joints, holding the float in a nearly vertical position. Continue applying grout and wiping off excess until about 25 sq ft. of the floor has been grouted.

Remove excess grout by wiping a damp sponge diagonally over about 2 sq ft. of the tile at a time. Rinse the sponge in cool water between wipes. Wipe each area only once. Continue this process until you've grouted all the joints. Allow the grout to dry for about 4 hours, then use a soft cloth to buff the tile surface and remove any remaining grout film.

After the grout has cured completely (check manufacturer's instructions), apply grout sealer to the grout lines using a small sponge brush. Don't brush sealer onto the tile surfaces, and wipe up any excess sealer immediately.

Installing Laminate Plank Floors

Laminate flooring comes in a floating system that is simple to install, even if you have little experience. You may install a floating laminate floor right on top of plywood or a concrete slab, or over sheet vinyl or even hardwood flooring. Just be sure to follow the manufacturer's instructions.

The pieces are available in planks or squares in a variety of different sizes, colors, and faux finishes—including wood and ceramic. The part you see is really a photographic print. Tongue-and-groove edges lock pieces together, and the entire floor floats on the underlayment. At the end of this project there are a few extra steps to take if your flooring manufacturer recommends using glue on the joints.

The rich wood tones of beautiful laminate planks may cause you to imagine hours of long, hard installation work, but this is a DIY project that you can do in a single weekend. Buy the manufactured planks at a home-improvement or flooring store and install laminate flooring with the step-by-step instructions offered in the following pages.

Tools & Materials ▸

Drill	Foam Insulation
Circular saw	Painter's tape
Hole saw	Chisel
Underlayment	Rubber mallet
½" spacers	Drawbar
Tapping block	Finish nails
Scrap foam	Nail set strap clamps
Speed square	Threshold and
Manufacturer glue	screws
Adhesive tape	Utility knife

Laminate strip flooring can be used very successfully in basements. When installed as a floating floor over an underlayment pad, it goes in quickly and is relatively inexpensive. See page 75 for suggestions on floor preparation.

How to Install a Floating Laminate Floor

To install the underlayment, start in one corner and unroll the underlayment to the opposite wall. Cut the underlayment to fit using a utility knife or scissors. Overlap the second underlayment sheet according to the manufacturer's recommendations, and secure the pieces in place with adhesive tape.

Working from the left corner of the room to the right, set ½" wall spacers and dry-lay planks (tongue side facing the wall) against the wall. The spacers allow for expansion. If you are flooring a room more than 26 ft. long or wide, you need to buy appropriate-sized expansion joints. *Note: Some manufacturers suggest facing the groove side to the wall.*

Final uncut plank
ends here

Set a new plank right-side up on top of the previously laid plank, flush with the spacer against the wall at the end run. Line up a speed square with the bottom plank edge and trace a line. That's the cutline for the final plank in the row.

Press painter's tape along the cutline on the top of the plank to prevent chips when cutting. Score the line drawn in step 3 with a utility knife. Turn the plank over and extend the pencil line to the backside.

(continued)

5

Clamp the board face down on rigid foam insulation or plywood to a work table. The foam reduces chipping. Clamp a speed square on top of the plank, as though you are going to draw another line parallel to the cutline—use this to eye your straight cut. Place the circular saw's blade on the waste side of the actual cutline.

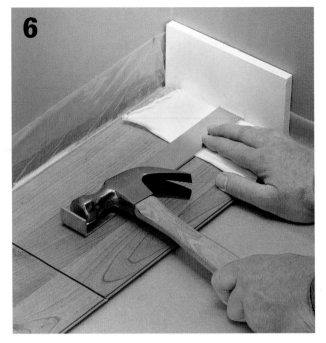

6

To create a tight fit for the last plank in the first row, place a spacer against the wall and wedge one end of a drawbar between it and the last plank. Tap the other end of the drawbar with a rubber mallet or hammer. Protect the laminate surface with a thin cloth.

7

Continue to lay rows of flooring, making sure the joints are staggered. This prevents the entire floor from relying on just a few joints, which keeps the planks from lifting. Staggering also stengthens the floor, because the joints are shorter and more evenly distributed.

8

To fit the final row, place two planks on top of the last course; slide the top plank up against the wall spacer. Use the top plank to draw a cutline lengthwise on the middle plank. Cut the middle plank to size using the same method as in Step 3, just across the grain. The very last board must be cut lengthwise and widthwise to fit.

How to Work Around Obstacles

Marking outside
edge of the pipe

Mark indicates
right outside edge
of the pipe

Position a plank end against the spacers on the wall next to the obstacle. Use a pencil to make two marks along the length of the plank indicating the points where the obstacle begins and ends.

Once the plank is snapped into the previous row, position the plank end against the obstacle. Make two marks with a pencil, this time on the end of the plank to indicate where the obstacle falls along the width of the board.

Use a speed square to extend the four lines. The space at which they intersect is the part of the plank that needs to be removed to make room for the obstacle to go through it. Use a drill with a Forstner bit, or a hole saw the same diameter as the space within the intersecting lines, and drill through the plank at the X. You'll be left with a hole; extend the cut to the edges with a jigsaw.

Install the plank by locking the tongue-and-groove joints with the preceding board. Fit the end piece in behind the pipe or obstacle. Apply manufacturer-recommended glue to the cut edges, and press the end piece tightly against the adjacent plank. Wipe away excess glue with a damp cloth.

Laying Resilient Tile Floors

As with any tile installation, resilient tile requires carefully positioned layout lines. Before committing to any layout and applying tile, conduct a dry run to identify potential problems.

Keep in mind the difference between reference lines (see opposite page) and layout lines. Reference lines mark the center of the room and divide it into quadrants. If the tiles don't lay out symmetrically along these lines, you'll need to adjust them slightly, creating layout lines. Once layout lines are established, installing the tile is a fairly quick process. Be sure to keep joints between the tiles tight and lay the tiles square.

Tiles with an obvious grain pattern can be laid so the grain of each tile is oriented identically throughout the installation. You can also use the quarter-turn method, in which each tile has its pattern grain running perpendicular to that of adjacent tiles. Whichever method you choose, be sure to be consistent throughout the project.

Tools & Materials ▸

Ceramic tile cutter
Tape measure
Chalk line
Framing square
Utility knife
1/16" notched trowel

Heat gun
Resilient tile
Flooring adhesive
  (for dry-back tile)
Metal threshold bars

Resilient tiles have a pattern layer that is bonded to a vinyl base and coated with a transparent wear layer. Some come with adhesive pre-applied and covered by a paper backing, others have dry backs and are designed to be set into flooring adhesive.

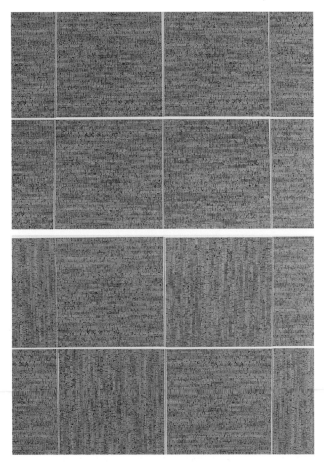

Check for noticeable directional features, like the grain of the vinyl particles. You can set the tiles in a running pattern so the directional feature runs in the same direction (top), or in a checkerboard pattern using the quarter-turn method (bottom).

How to Make Reference Lines for Tile Installation

Position a reference line (X) by measuring along opposite sides of the room and marking the center of each side. Snap a chalk line between these marks.

Measure and mark the centerpoint of the chalk line. From this point, use a framing square to establish a second reference line perpendicular to the first one. Snap the second line (Y) across the room.

Check the reference lines for squareness using the 3-4-5 triangle method. Measure along reference line X and make a mark 3 ft. from the centerpoint. Measure from the centerpoint along reference line Y and make a mark at 4 ft.

Measure the distance between the marks. If the reference lines are perpendicular, the distance will measure exactly 5 ft. If not, adjust the reference lines until they're exactly perpendicular to each other.

How to Install Dry-backed Resilient Tile

Snap perpendicular reference lines with a chalk line (see page 101). Dry-fit tiles along layout line Y so a joint falls along reference line X. If necessary, shift the layout to make the layout symmetrical or to reduce the number of tiles that need to be cut.

If you shift the tile layout, create a new line that is parallel to reference line X and runs through a tile joint near line X. The new line, X1, is the line you'll use when installing the tile. Use a different colored chalk to distinguish between lines.

Dry-fit tiles along the new line, X1. If necessary, adjust the layout line as in steps 1 and 2.

If you adjusted the layout along X1, measure and make a new layout line, Y1, that's parallel to reference line Y and runs through a tile joint. Y1 will form the second layout line you'll use during installation.

5

Apply adhesive around the intersection of the layout lines using a trowel with 1/16" V-shaped notches. Hold the trowel at a 45° angle and spread adhesive evenly over the surface.

6

Spread adhesive over most of the installation area, covering three quadrants. Allow the adhesive to set according to the manufacturer's instructions, then begin to install the tile at the intersection of the layout lines. You can kneel on installed tiles to lay additional tiles.

7

When the first three quadrants are completely tiled, spread adhesive over the remaining quadrant, then finish setting the tile.

8

To cut tiles to fit along the walls, place the tile to be cut (A) face up on top of the last full tile you installed. Position a 1/8"-thick spacer against the wall, then set a marker tile (B) on top of the tile to be cut. Trace along the edge of the marker tile to draw a cutting line.

(continued)

Marking Corners ▸

9

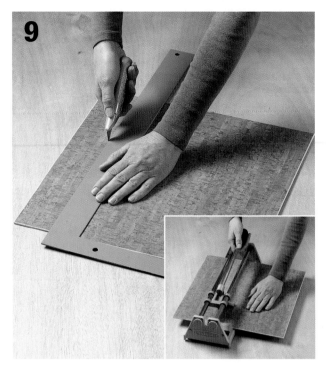

To mark tiles for cutting around outside corners, make a cardboard template to match the space, keeping a ⅛" gap along the walls. After cutting the template, check to make sure it fits. Place the template on a tile and trace its outline.

Cut tile to fit using a utility knife and straightedge. Hold the straightedge securely against the cutting line to ensure a straight cut. *Option: You can use a ceramic-tile cutter to make straight cuts in thick vinyl tiles (see inset).*

10

11

Install cut tiles next to the walls. If you're precutting all tiles before installing them, measure the distance between the wall and the last row of tiles. Install tiles at various points in case the distance changes.

Continue installing tile in the remaining quadrants until the room is completely covered. Check the entire floor. If you find loose areas, press down on the tiles to bond them to the underlayment. Install metal threshold bars at room borders where the new floor joins another floor covering.

Variation: Self-adhesive Resilient Tile

Once your reference lines are established (see page 101), peel off the paper backing and install the first tile in one of the corners formed by the intersecting layout lines. Lay three or more tiles along each layout lines in the quadrant. Rub the entire surface of each tile to bond the adhesive to the floor underlayment.

Begin installing tiles in the interior area of the quadrant. Keep the joints tight between tiles..

Finish setting full tiles in the first quadrant, then set the full tiles in an adjacent quadrant. Set the tiles along the layout lines first, then fill in the interior tiles.

Continue installing the tile in the remaining quadrants until the room is completely covered. Check the entire floor. If you find loose areas, press down on the tiles to bond them to the underlayment. Install metal threshold bars at room borders where the new floor joins another floor covering.

Installing Rubber Roll Floors

Once a mark of restaurants and retailers, sheet rubber flooring has become an option for homeowners as well. It's resilient, durable, and stable, holding up well under the heaviest and most demanding use. Better still, it's comfortable to walk on and easy to maintain.

The durability and resilience of rubber provide benefits in two ways. First, the flooring takes just about any kind of use without showing damage. Second, it absorbs shock in proportion to its thickness. Heavier rubber floors help prevent fatigue, making them comfortable for standing, walking, and even strenuous exercise.

Many new flooring products are made from recycled rubber, which saves landfill space and reduces the consumption of new raw materials. This is one place a petroleum-based product is environmentally friendly.

To install rubber sheet flooring on top of wood, use only exterior-grade plywood, one side sanded. Do not use lauan plywood, particleboard, chipboard, or hardboard. Make sure the surface is level, smooth, and securely fastened to the subfloor.

Tools & Materials ▸

Adhesive	Mineral spirits
Chalk line	Notched trowel
Cleaning supplies	Painter's tape
Craft/utility knife	Straightedge
Flat-edged trowel	Weighted roller
Measuring tape	

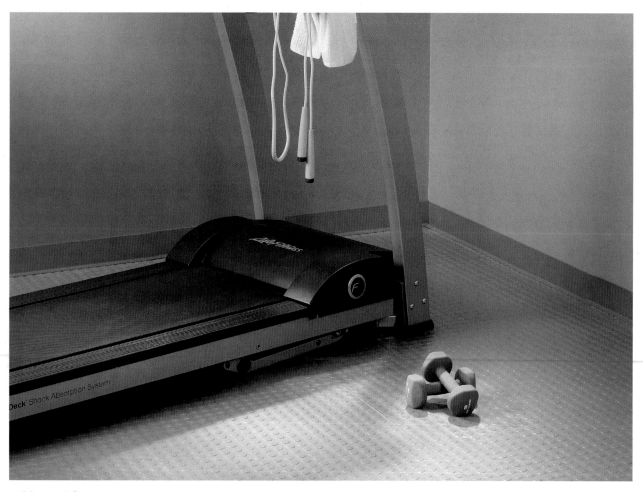

Rubber roll flooring resists water damage, provides cushion underfoot and has a warm feeling.

How to Install Rubber Roll Flooring

Mark the first strip of rubber roll flooring for cutting to length. Start on the longest wall, and mark the cutting line so the strip will be a couple of inches too long. Use a straightedge guide to mark the cutting lines, and then cut with a sharp utility knife (be sure to put a backer board under the material before cutting it).

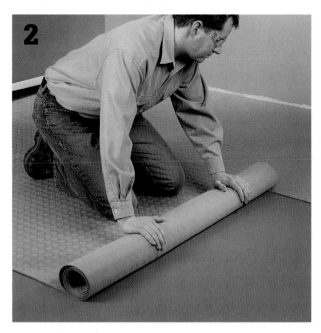

Set the first strip against the long wall so the overage in length is equal at each end. Cut the next strip to length and then butt it up against the first strip. Adjust the second strip so it overlaps the first strip by 1 to 1½ inches, making sure the strips remain parallel. Lay out all of the strips in the room in this manner.

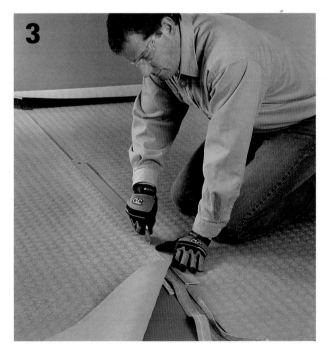

Cut the strips to create perfectly matched seams. With a backer board underneath the seam, center a straightedge on the top strip and carefully cut through both strips in the overlap area. Change utility knife blades frequently, and don't try to make the cut in one pass unless your flooring is very thin.

Remove the waste material from the seam area and test the fit of the strips. Because they were cut together, they should align perfectly. Make sure you don't adjust the position of one of the strips or the seams may not align properly.

(continued)

Fold back one half of the first strip so half of the flooring subbase is exposed. Again, take care not to shift the position of the flooring strip.

Apply the adhesive recommended by the flooring manufacturer to the exposed floor, using a notched trowel. Avoid getting adhesive on the surface of the flooring, and make sure the adhesive is applied all the way up to the walls and just past the seam area.

Lower the roll slowly onto the adhesive, making sure not to allow any air to become trapped underneath. Never leave adhesive ridges or puddles; they will become visible on the surface.

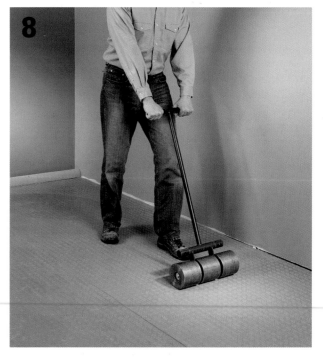

Roll the floor immediately with a 100-pound roller to squeeze out any trapped air and maximize contact between the roll and the adhesive. With each pass of the roller, overlap the previous pass by half. Roll the width first, then the length, and re-roll after 30 minutes.

9

Fold back the second half of the first roll and the first half of the second roll. Apply and spread the adhesive as before. Spread the adhesive at a 90° angle to the seams. This will reduce the chance of having adhesive squeeze up through the seams. Continue installing strips in this manner.

10

Clean up adhesive squeezeout or spills immediately using a rag and mineral spirits. At seams, take care not to allow mineral spirits to get underneath the flooring, as it will ruin the adhesive.

11

Press down on any bubbles or on seams that do not have a seamless appearance. If a seam resists lying flat, set a board and weights over it overnight. It is a good idea to hand-roll all seams with a J-roller, in addition to rolling the entire floor with a floor roller.

12

Trim off excess flooring at the ends using a utility knife. Leaving a slight gap between the flooring and the wall is fine as long as you plan to install base molding.

Laying Carpet

Carpet remains one of the most popular and versatile of all floor coverings. Almost every home has wall-to-wall carpet in at least a few rooms. It's available in an almost endless variety of colors, styles, and patterns. It can also be custom made to express a more personal design. Most carpet is nylon based, although acrylic and polyester are also popular. Wool carpeting is more formal and more expensive but also quite popular. All are suitable for a basement installation, but avoid carpet with a thick pile.

Part of carpet's appeal is its soft texture. It's pleasant to walk on—especially with bare feet, since it's soft and warm underfoot—and comfortable for children to play on. It is a great way to warm up a cold basement floor. Because carpet has a pad underneath that acts as a cushion, carpet can help reduce "floor fatigue."

Wall-to-wall carpet is usually installed with a pad beneath it, although some is sold with a preattached foam pad. Carpet with a preattached pad tends to be of lesser quality, but some prefer it for basements

because it does not require stretching and tacking so it can be removed quickly if need be and reinstalled with little difficulty. If you are installing a carpet pad, choose one that is made of waffle-pattern rubber rather than one that is fiber-based (the less absorbent the pad is, the better).

Tools & Materials ▶

Measuring tape	Chalk line
Seam iron	Knee-kicker
Edge trimmer	Scissors
Hammer	Seam tape
Aviation strips	Double-sided carpet
Stapler	tape
Duct tape	Tackless strips
Utlity knife	Carpet padding
Power stretcher	

Carpet does have some disadvantages in basements, but for warming up and softening a cold concrete floor, it is the best game in town. This makes it a very popular basement flooring option.

Buying & Estimating Carpet

When choosing carpet, one thing to consider is color and pattern. Lighter shades and colors show dirt and stains more readily, but they provide an open, spacious feel. Darker colors and multicolored patterns don't show as much dirt or wear, but they can also make a room appear smaller.

The materials used in a carpet and its construction can affect the carpet's durability. In high-traffic areas, such as hallways and entryways, a top-quality fiber will last longer. Carpet construction, the way in which fibers are attached to the backing, impacts resistance to wear and appearance.

Available widths of certain carpets may affect your buying decision; a roll that's wide enough to cover an entire room eliminates the need for seaming. When seaming is unavoidable, calculate the total square footage to be covered, then add 20 percent to cover trimming and seaming.

The type of carpet will dictate the type of pad you should use. Check carpet sample labels for the manufacturer's recommendations. Since carpet and padding work in tandem to create a floor covering system, use the best pad you can afford that works with your carpet. In addition to making your carpet feel more plush underfoot, the pad makes your floor quieter and warmer. A high-quality pad also helps reduce carpet wear.

Tips for Evaluating Carpet ▶

Fiber Type	Characteristics
Nylon	Easy to clean, very durable, good stain resistance; colors sometimes fade in direct sunlight
Polyester	Excellent stain resistance, very soft in thick cut-pile constructions; colors don't fade in sunlight
Olefin	Virtually stain- and fade-proof, resists moisture and static; not as resilient as nylon or as soft as polyester
Acrylic	Resembles wool in softness and look, good moisture resistance; less durable than other synthetics
Wool	Luxurious look and feel, good durability and warmth; more costly and less stain-resistant than synthetics

Labels on the back of samples usually tell you the fiber composition, the available widths (usually 12 or 15 feet), what antistain treatments and other finishes were applied, and details of the product warranty.

Planning for Carpet Installation

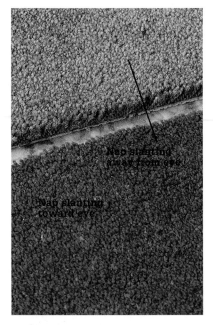

Keep pile direction consistent.
Carpet pile is usually slanted, which affects how the carpet looks from different angles as light reflects off the surface. Place seamed pieces so the pile faces the same direction.

Maintain patterns when seaming patterned carpet. Because of this necessity, there's always more waste when installing patterned carpet. For a pattern that repeats itself every 18", for example, each piece must be oversized 18" to ensure the pattern is aligned. Pattern repeat measurements are noted on carpet samples.

At seams, add an extra 3" to each piece when estimating the amount of carpet you'll need. This extra material helps when cutting straight edges for seaming.

Add 6" for each edge that's along the wall. This surplus will be trimmed away when the carpet is cut to the exact size of the room.

Measure from the closet wall to the closet door. Closet floors are usually covered with a separate piece of carpet that's seamed to the carpet in the main room area.

How to Install Carpet

Starting in a corner, nail tackless strips to the floor, keeping a gap between the strips and the walls that's about ⅔ the thickness of the carpet. Use plywood spacers. Angled pins on the strip should point toward the wall.

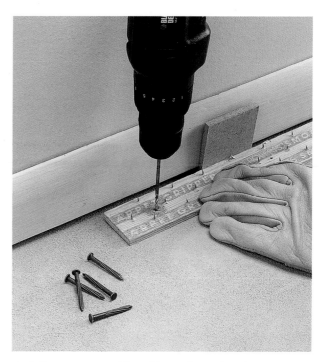

Variation: Use extrawide tackless strips and masonry anchors if installing carpet directly to a concrete floor without underlayment. Typically this method is not recommended unless your basement floor is exceptionally dry and well sealed.

Roll out enough padding to cover the entire floor. Make sure the seams between the padding are tight. If one face of the padding has a slicker surface, keep the slick surface face up, making it easier to slide the carpet over the pad during installation.

Use a utility knife to cut away excess padding along the edges. The padding should touch but not overlap the tackless strips.

(continued)

4

Tape the seams together with duct tape, then staple the padding to the floor every 12".

Variation: To fasten padding to a concrete floor, apply double-sided tape next to the tackless strips, along the seams, and in an X pattern across the floor.

5

Position the carpet roll against one wall, with its loose end extending up the wall about 6", then roll out the carpet until it reaches the opposite wall.

6

At the opposite wall, mark the back of the carpet at each edge about 6" beyond the point where the carpet touches the wall. Pull the carpet back away from the wall so the marks are visible.

7

Snap a chalk line across the back of the carpet between the marks. Place a scrap piece of plywood under the cutting area to protect the carpet and padding from the knife blade. Cut along the line using a straightedge and utility knife.

8

Next to walls, straddle the edge of the carpet and nudge it with your foot until it extends up the wall by about 6" and is parallel to the wall.

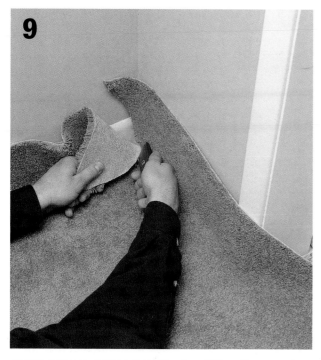

9

At the corners, relieve buckling by slitting the carpet with a utility knife, allowing the carpet to lie somewhat flat. Make sure that corner cuts do not cut into usable carpet.

10

Using your seaming plan as a guide, measure and cut fill-in pieces of carpet to complete the installation. Be sure to include a 6" surplus at each wall and a 3" surplus on each edge that will be seamed to another piece of carpet. Set the cut pieces in place, making sure the pile faces in the same direction on all pieces.

(continued)

Roll back the large piece of carpet on the side to be seamed, then use a chalk line to snap a straight seam edge about 2" from the factory edge. Keep the ends of the line about 18" from the sides of the carpet where the overlap onto the walls causes the carpet to buckle.

Using a straightedge and utility knife, carefully cut the carpet along the chalk line. To extend the cutting lines to the edges of the carpet, pull the corners back at an angle so they lie flat, then cut the line with the straightedge and utility knife. Place scrap wood under the cutting area to protect the carpet while cutting.

On smaller carpet pieces, cut straight seam edges where the small pieces will be joined to one another. Don't cut the edges that will be seamed to the large carpet piece until after the small pieces are joined together.

Plug in the seam iron and set it aside to heat up, then measure and cut hot-glue seam tape for all seams. Begin by joining the small fill-in pieces to form one large piece. Center the tape under the seam with the adhesive side facing up.

Set the iron under the carpet at one end of the tape until the adhesive liquifies, usually about 30 seconds. Working in 12" sections, slowly move the iron along the tape, letting the carpet fall onto the hot adhesive behind it. Set weights at the end of the seam to hold the pieces in place.

Press the edges of the carpet together into the melted adhesive behind the iron. Separate the pile with your fingers to make sure no fibers are stuck in the glue and the seam is tight, then place a weighted board over the seam to keep it flat while the glue sets.

Continue seaming the fill-in pieces together. When the tape adhesive has dried, turn the seamed piece over and cut a fresh seam edge as done in step 7. Reheat and remove about 1½" of tape from the end of each seam to keep it from overlapping the tape on the large piece.

(continued)

18

Use hot-glue seam tape to join the seamed pieces to the large piece of carpet, repeating steps 14 through 17.

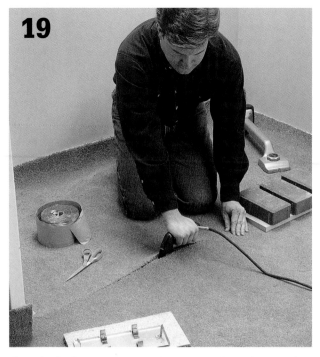

19

If you're laying carpet in a closet, cut a fill-in piece and join it to the main carpet with hot-glue seam tape.

20

Before stretching the seamed carpet, read through this entire section and create a stretching sequence similar to the one shown here. Start by fastening the carpet at a doorway threshold using carpet transitions.

21

If the doorway is close to a corner, use the knee kicker to secure the carpet to the tackless strips between the door and the corner. Also secure a few feet of carpet along the adjacent wall, working toward the corner.

22

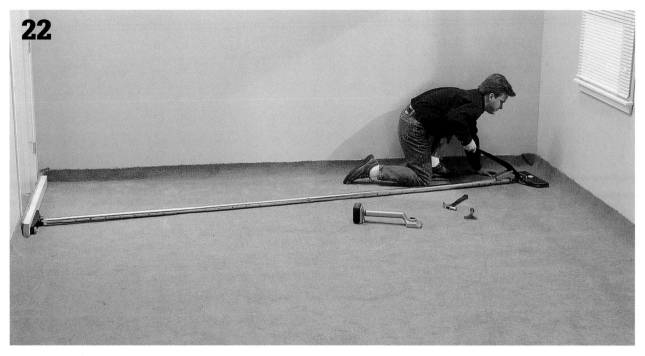

Use a power stretcher to stretch the carpet toward the wall opposite the door. Brace the tail with a length of 2 × 4 placed across the doorway. Leaving the tail in place and moving only the stretcher head, continue stretching and securing the carpet along the wall, working toward the nearest corner in 12 to 24" increments.

23

As you stretch the carpet, secure it onto the tackless strips with a stair tool and hammer.

24

With the power stretcher still extended from the doorway to the opposite side of the room, knee-kick the carpet onto the tackless strips along the closest wall, starting near the corner closest to the stretcher tail. Disengage and move the stretcher only if it's in the way.

(continued)

25

Reposition the stretcher so its tail is against the center of the wall you just secured. Stretch and secure the carpet along the opposite wall, working from the center toward a corner. If there's a closet in an adjacent wall, work toward that wall, not the closet.

26

Use the knee kicker to stretch and secure the carpet inside the closet (if any). Stretch and fasten the carpet against the back wall first, then do the side walls. After the carpet in the closet is stretched and secured, use the knee kicker to secure the carpet along the walls next to the closet. Disengage the power stretcher only if it's in the way.

27

Return the head of the power stretcher to the center of the wall. Finish securing carpet along this wall, working toward the other corner of the room.

28

Reposition the stretcher to secure the carpet along the last wall of the room, working from the center toward the corners. The tail block should be braced against the opposite wall.

29

Use a carpet edge trimmer to trim surplus carpet away from the walls. At corners, use a utility knife to finish the cuts.

30

Tuck the trimmed edges of the carpet neatly into the gaps between the tackless strips and the walls using a stair tool and hammer.

Walls & Ceilings

Basement walls should be hard surfaced for easy cleaning and built from materials that do not promote mold growth. Most wallboard manufacturers now make mold-resistant panels that cost only about 50 percent more than standard wallboard. It is a minimal investment and very cheap insurance against air-quality problems and other negative effects of mold.

Basement ceilings should also be made using mold-resistant materials. This can include wallboard, which is a very common ceiling material used throughout the house. But even acoustic panels and suspended ceilings are now available with panels that don't promote mold. Because of the frequent need for access to ductwork, plumbing, gas lines, and wiring in the basement ceiling joists, suspended ceilings with their removable panels are very popular in basement remodeling.

Framing for basement walls can be standard 2× lumber, but if you have had moisture problems in your basement, consider using metal studs instead. Any wood framing members that are in contact with the concrete floor or concrete walls should be made from pressure-treated lumber.

In this chapter:

Wall & Ceiling Options

Framing walls and ceilings is done in pretty much the same manner in basements as in the other parts of the house. Although not required, it is a good idea to use pressure-treated lumber to make the sole plates for walls if they are resting directly on the concrete floor. Otherwise, not much is different. The choices for covering framed walls are also much the same as anywhere else. If covering your walls with wallboard, use newer mold-resistant material in a damp basement environment. In general, avoid using materials that encourage mold growth, especially on walls. These include wallpapers and most paneling sheets.

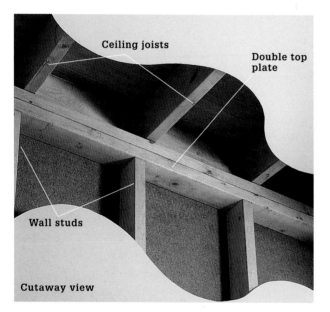

Load-bearing walls carry the structural weight of your home. In platform-framed houses, load-bearing walls can be identified by double top plates made from two layers of framing lumber. Load-bearing walls include all exterior walls and any interior walls that are aligned above support beams.

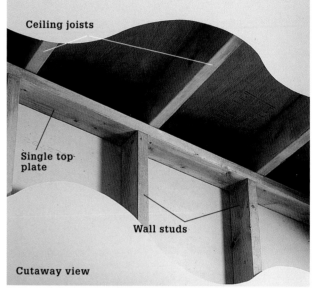

Nonloadbearing walls are interior walls that do not carry the structural weight of the house. They have a single top plate and can be perpendicular to the floor and ceiling joists but are not aligned above support beams. Any interior wall that is parallel to floor and ceiling joists is a partition wall.

Moisture- and mold-resistant wallboard (top) should be used to cover basement walls and ceilings. Some of these new products are paperless, which eliminates the primary source of food for mold and mildew. Standard wallboard (middle) is best for upper level installations, although in dry basements you can probably us it safely on ceilings. Greenboard (bottom) is standard wallboard that has a moisture-resistant vinyl coating rather than paper. Often used for shower panel backer, it is a better choice for walls than standard material but more likely to develop mold and moisture problems than paperless.

Wall Types

Walls built against foundation walls typically are framed with furring strips to support the wallcoverings. This type of wall is tricky to plan and has some potential problems. Read the section on insulating your basement for an important discussion of the intricacies of building against a foundation wall (see pages 128 to 129).

Partition walls divide large spaces, such as basements, into smaller living spaces. They are framed with standard construction grade 2 x 4s or with metal studs.

Panelized basement wall systems feature removable fabric-covered panels that are installed in tracks. A little reminiscent of office cubicle walls, the panels provide some insulation value and are mold and moisture resistant. They typically are available through franchise installers.

Ceiling Types

Wallboard is an inexpensive covering for basement ceilings, but it has the limitation of not being easily removed if you need access to any ductwork or utilities in the ceiling joist cavities.

Suspended ceilings and acoustic tile ceilings have panels that can be removed to create access to elements in the joist cavities, but they do lower the ceiling height a few inches. Be sure to shop for panels that are mold resistant.

Powder-Actuated Tools ▸

Basement floors and walls are almost always made of concrete or concrete products, which can present some difficulty when it comes time to attach walls. You can use hardened masonry screws for fastening, but that involves lots of tedious drilling and usually a few broken or stripped screw heads. An easier alternative is to use small charges of gunpowder to drive hardened nails into metal or concrete with a powder-actuated nail gun.

Powder-actuated nailers look and work a bit like a pile driver or handgun. A steel barrel holds specially designed hardened nails called drive pins. The nails are equipped with a plastic sleeve to keep them centered in the barrel. Driving force is delivered by a small gunpowder charge, called a power load, which looks like a rifle shell with a crimped tip. The power loads fit into a magazine behind the barrel on the tool. Squeezing the tool's trigger, or hitting the end with a hammer (depending on the tool style), activates a firing pin that ignites the gunpowder. The expanding gasses drive a piston against the nail at great force. Powder-actuated nailers can drive only one fastener at a time, but some styles will hold a clip of multiple power loads for faster operation.

Power loads are made in a range of color-coded calibers to suit different nailing applications and drive pin sizes. Follow the manufacturer's recommendations carefully to choose the correct load and fastener for your task. Generally, the safest method is to start with the lowest energy load that will work for your nailing situation and see if it's sufficient to fully drive the nail. Use the next stronger load, if necessary.

Powder-actuated nailers are easy to use for do-it-yourselfers and safe for indoor projects, provided you wear hearing and eye protection and follow all manufacturer's instructions. Most home centers sell the nail guns and supplies, or you can rent these tools.

Powder-actuated nailers offer the quickest and easiest method for fastening framing to block, poured concrete, and steel.

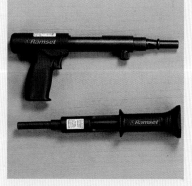

Powder-actuated nail guns (PATs) are designed in two styles. Plunger types are activated by hitting the end of the shaft with a hammer, while trigger styles function like a handgun. With either type, the barrel must be depressed against the work surface to release a safety before a drive pin can be fired.

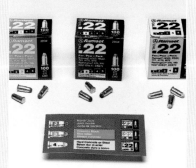

Power loads contain various amounts of gunpowder inside a crimped shell. Color coding ensures that you're using the right amount of charge for your drive pin size and the materials you're fastening together. Follow the color charts carefully, starting with a low-power charge.

PATs use hardened nails, called drive pins, in a range of sizes. A plastic finned sleeve centers the drive pin in the tool barrel.

How to Use a PAT

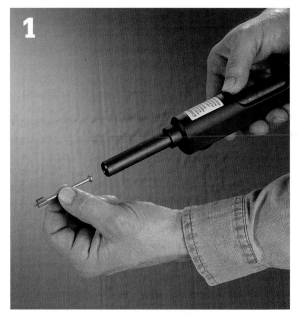

To prepare a PAT for use, slide a drive pin into the barrel first. Push it in until the nail tip is flush with the end of the barrel. Be sure there's no power load in the magazine.

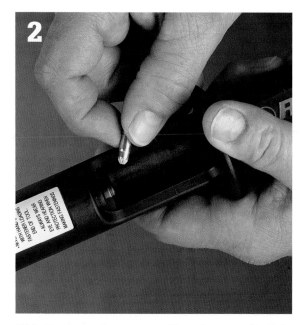

Slide the magazine open and insert a power load into the barrel. A rim on the load shell ensures that it can only be loaded one way. Close the magazine.

Press the end of the barrel firmly against the work surface to release the safety. Squeeze the trigger or strike the end of the tool sharply with a hammer to fire the drive pin. Once the pin is fired, slide open the magazine to eject the spent load shell.

Driving Nails ▸

Occasionally, your first power load selection won't completely set the nail. In this situation, use a hand maul to drive it in the rest of the way. Choose a stronger power load for driving subsequent fasteners.

Framing Furred-Out Walls

Wall framing members can be attached directly to a concrete foundation wall to provide a support for wall coverings and to house wires and pipes. Because they have no significant structural purpose, they are usually made with smaller stock called furring strips, which can be 2 × 2 or 2 × 3 wood. Do not install furring strips in conjunction with a vapor barrier or insulation, and do not attach them to walls that are not dry walls (see definition, page 43) with insulation on the exterior side.

Furring strips serve primarily to create nailing surfaces for wallboard. Attach them to dry basement walls at web locations of block wall where possible.

How to Attach Furring Strips to Dry Foundation Walls

Cut a 2 × 2 top plate to span the length of the wall. Mark the furring-strip layout onto the bottom edge of the plate using 16"-on-center spacing. Attach the plate to the bottom of the joists with 2½" wallboard screws. The back edge of the plate should line up with the front of the blocks.

If the joists run parallel to the wall, you'll need to install backers between the outer joist and the sill plate to provide support for ceiling wallboard. Make T-shaped backers from short 2 × 4s and 2 × 2s. Install each so the bottom face of the 2 × 4 is flush with the bottom edge of the joists. Attach the top plate to the foundation wall with its top edge flush with the top of the blocks.

3

Install a bottom plate cut from pressure-treated 2 × 2 lumber so the plate spans the length of the wall. Apply construction adhesive to the back and bottom of the plate, then attach it to the floor with a nailer. Use a plumb bob to transfer the furring-strip layout marks from the top plate to the bottom plate.

4

Cut 2 × 2 furring strips to fit between the top and bottom plates. Apply construction adhesive to the back of each furring strip, and position it on the layout marks on the plates. Nail along the length of each strip at 16" intervals.

5

Option: Leave a channel for the installation of wires or supply pipes by installing pairs of vertically aligned furring strips with a 2" gap between each pair. *Note: Consult local codes to ensure proper installation of electrical or plumbing materials.*

Isolate the Wall ▸

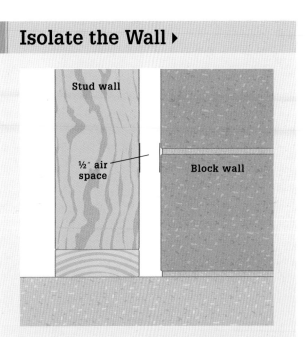

Stud wall

½" air space

Block wall

It consumes more floorspace, but a good alternative to a furred-out wall is to build a 2 x 4 stud wall parallel to the foundation wall, but ½" away from it. This eliminates any contact between the wall framing members and the foundation wall. See pages 130 to 132 for instructions on building a partition wall.

Building Partition Walls

Non-loadbearing, or partition, walls are typically built with 2 × 4 lumber and are supported by ceiling or floor joists above or by blocking between the joists. For basement walls that sit on bare concrete, use pressure-treated lumber for the bottom plates.

This project shows you how to build a wall in place, rather than how to build a complete wall on the floor and tilt it upright, as in new construction. The build-in-place method allows for variations in floor and ceiling levels and is generally much easier for remodeling projects.

If your wall will include a door or other opening, see pages 134 and 135 before laying out the wall. *Note: After your walls are framed and the mechanical rough-ins are completed, be sure to install metal protector plates where pipes and wires run through framing members.*

Tools & Materials ▸

Saw	Fiberglass sealant
Chalk line	2 × 4 lumber
Circular saw	Blocking lumber
Framing square	10d, 16d, and 8d
Plumb bob	common nails
Powder-actuated nailer	Concrete fasteners
T-bevel	Wallboard screws
Measuring tape	Acoustic sealant
Hammer	Masonry screws

A typical partition wall consists of top and bottom plates and 2 × 4 studs spaced 16" on center top. Use 2 × 6 lumber for walls that will hold large plumbing pipes (bottom).

Variations for Fastening Top Plates to Joists

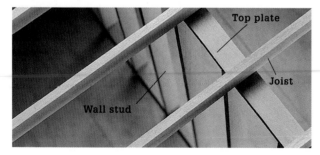

When a new wall is perpendicular to the ceiling or floor joists above, attach the top plate directly to the joists, using 16d nails.

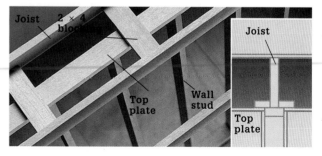

When a new wall falls between parallel joists, install 2 × 4 blocking between the joists every 24". If the new wall is aligned with a parallel joist, install blocks on both sides of the wall, and attach the top plate to the joist (inset).

How to Build a Partition Wall

Mark the location of the leading edge of the new wall's top plate, then snap a chalk line through the marks across the joists or blocks. Use a framing square or take measurements to make sure the line is perpendicular to any intersecting walls. Cut the top and bottom plates to length.

Set the plates together with their ends flush. Measure from the end of one plate, and make marks for the location of each stud. The first stud should fall 15¼" from the end; every stud thereafter should fall 16" on center. Thus, the first 4 × 8–ft. wallboard panel will cover the first stud and "break" in the center of the fourth stud. Use a square to extend the marks across both plates. Draw an X at each stud location.

Position the top plate against the joists, aligning its leading edge with the chalk line. Attach the plate with two 16d nails driven into each joist. Start at one end and adjust the plate as you go to keep the leading edge flush with the chalk line.

To position the bottom plate, hang a plumb bob from the side edge of the top plate so the point nearly touches the floor. When it hangs motionless, mark the point's location on the floor. Make plumb markings at each end of the top plate, then snap a chalk line between the marks. Position the bottom plate along the chalk line and use the plumb bob to align the stud markings between the two plates.

(continued)

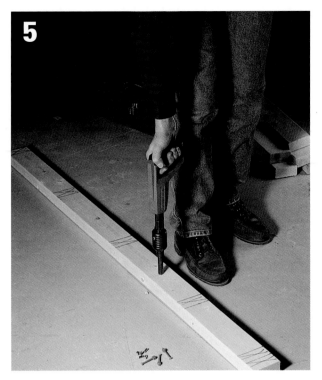

Fasten the bottom plate to the floor. On concrete, use a powder-actuated nailer or masonry screws, driving a pin or screw every 16". On wood floors, use 16d nails driven into the joists or sleepers below.

Measure between the plates for the length of each stud. Cut each stud so it fits snugly in place but is not so tight that it bows the joists above. If you cut a stud too short, see if it will fit somewhere else down the wall.

Install the studs by toenailing them at a 60° angle through the sides of the studs and into the plates. At each end, drive two 8d nails through one side of the stud and one more through the center on the other side.

Option: If building codes in your area require fire blocking, install 2× cutoff scraps between the studs 4 ft. from the floor to serve this purpose. Stagger the blocks so you can endnail each piece.

Options for Framing Corners

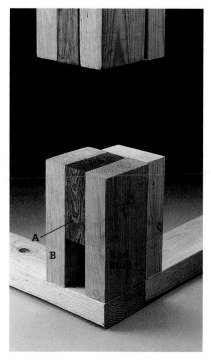

L-corners: Nail 2 × 4 spacers (A) to the inside of the end stud. Nail an extra stud (B) to the spacers. The extra stud provides a surface to attach wallboard at the inside corner.

T-corner meets stud: Fasten 2 × 2 backers (A) to each side of the side-wall stud (B). The backers provide a nailing surface for wallboard.

T-corner between studs: Fasten a 1 × 6 backer (A) to the end stud (B) with wallboard screws. The backer provides a nailing surface for wallboard.

How to Build a Soundproofed Partition Wall

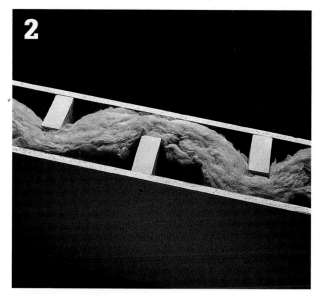

Frame new partition walls using 2 × 6 plates. Space the studs 12" apart, staggering them so alternate studs are aligned with opposite sides of the plates. Seal under and above the plates with acoustic sealant.

Weave R-11 unfaced fiberglass blanket insulation horizontally between the studs. Cover each side with one or more layers of ⅝" mold-resistant drywall.

How to Frame Door Openings

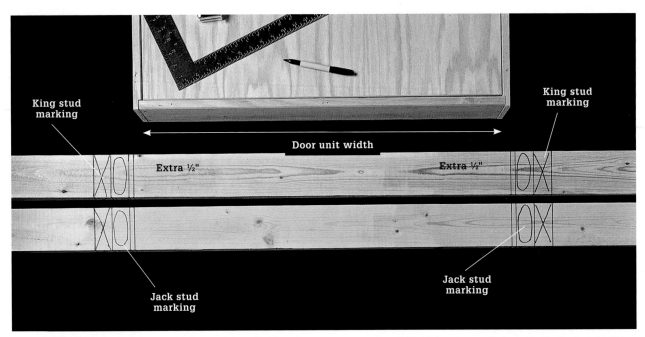

King stud marking

King stud marking

Door unit width

Extra ½"

Extra ½"

Jack stud marking

Jack stud marking

To mark the layout for the studs that make up the door frame, measure the width of the door unit along the bottom. Add 1" to this dimension to calculate the width of the rough opening (the distance between the jack studs). This gives you a ½" gap on each side for adjusting the door frame during installation. Mark the top and bottom plates for the jack and king studs.

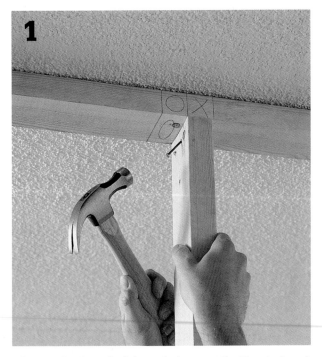

After you've installed the wall plates, cut the king studs and toenail them in place at the appropriate markings.

Measure the full length of the door unit, then add ½" to determine the height of the rough opening. Using that dimension, measure up from the floor and mark the king studs. Cut a 2 × 4 header to fit between the king studs. Position the header flat, with its bottom face at the marks, and secure it to the king studs with 16d nails.

3

Cut and install a cripple stud above the header centered between the king studs. Install any additional cripples required to maintain the 16"-on-center layout of the standard studs in the rest of the wall.

4

Cut the jack studs to fit snugly under the header. Fasten them in place by nailing down through the header, then drive 10d nails through the faces of the jack studs and into the king studs

Option: Build a header from two pieces of 2 × 4 or 2 × 6, sandwiching a strip of ½" plywood. Structural headers are required in load-bearing walls, but it is very unlikely that you'll be creating new load-bearing walls in your basement. Still, if you are a fan of overbuilding, the header will create a sturdier wall.

5

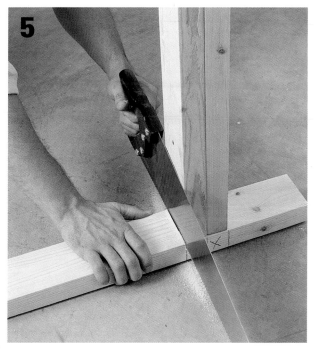

Saw through the bottom plate so it's flush with the inside faces of the jack studs. Remove the cut-out portion of the plate. *Note: If the wall will be finished with wallboard, hang the door after the wallboard is installed.*

Framing Walls with Steel Studs

Steel framing is quickly becoming a popular alternative to wood in residential construction due to the rising cost of wood and the advantages that steel offers. Steel framing is fireproof, insect proof, highly rot resistant, and lightweight. But the most significant advantage is that steel, unlike lumber, is always perfectly uniform and straight.

Steel studs and tracks (or plates) are commonly available at home centers and lumberyards in nominal widths comparable to their wooden counterparts: 1⅝" (2 × 2), 2½" (2 × 3), 3⅝" (2 × 4), and 5½" (2 × 6). Although 25-gauge (or 18-mil) and 20-gauge (or 33-mil) steel framing is suitable for most non-load-bearing partition walls and soffits that will be covered with wallboard, 20-gauge results in a somewhat sturdier wall. Use 20-gauge studs for walls that will receive cementboard.

With a few exceptions, the layout and framing methods used for a steel-frame partition wall are the same as those used for a wood-frame wall. For more information on framing partition walls, see pages 130 to 133; for help with framing soffits, see pages 140 to 141.

Here are a few tips for working with steel:

• Steel framing is fastened together with screws, not nails. Attach steel tracks to existing wood framing using long drywall screws.

• Even pressure and slow drill speed make it easy to start screws. Drive the screws down tight, but be careful not to strip the steel. Don't use drill-point screws with 25-gauge steel, which can strip easily.

• Most steel studs have punch-outs for running plumbing and electrical lines through the framing. Cut the studs to length from the same end to keep the punch-outs lined up.

• The hand-cut edges of steel framing are very sharp; wear heavy gloves when handling them.

• To provide support for electrical receptacle boxes, use boxes with special bracing for steel studs, or fasten boxes to wood framing installed between the studs.

• Use 16"-wide batts for insulating between steel studs. The added width allows for a friction fit, whereas standard batts would slide down.

Steel framing, when coupled with wallboard, creates a rigid wall system as solid and strong as wood-framed walls. Steel track is used to create plates, headers, and sills. Steel studs are installed so the open side faces in the same direction, except at door, window, or other openings. The punch-outs in studs are for running utility lines through the framing.

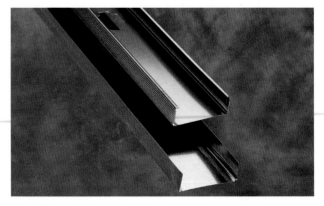

Steel studs and tracks have the same basic structure—a web that spans two flange sides—however, studs also contain a ¼" lip to improve their rigidity.

Tools & Materials ▸

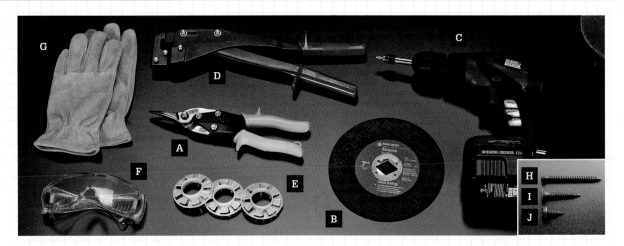

Steel framing requires a few specialty tools and materials. Aviation snips (A) are needed to cut tracks and studs, though a miter saw outfitted with a steel-cutting abrasive blade (B) can speed up the process. A drill or screwgun (C) is required for fastening framing. Handy for large projects, a stud crimper (D) creates mechanical joints between tracks and studs. Plastic grommets (E) are placed in punch-outs to help protected gas and power lines. Protective eyewear and heavy work gloves (F, G) are necessities when working with hand-cut steel framing. Use self-tapping screws (inset) to fasten steel components. To install wood trim, use Type S trim head screws (H); to fasten wallboard, Type S wallboard screws (I); and to fasten studs and tracks together, 7/16" Type S panhead screws (J).

Tips for Framing with Steel ▸

When running metal plumbing pipe and electrical cable through steel studs, use plastic grommets at punch-outs to prevent galvanic action and electrification of the wall. Install wood blocking between studs for hanging decorative accessories or wainscoting.

Fastening tab

Frame door openings 3" wider and 1½" taller than normal, then wrap the insides with 2 × 4s to provide a nailing surface for hanging the door and installing the casing.

How to Frame Walls with Steel Studs

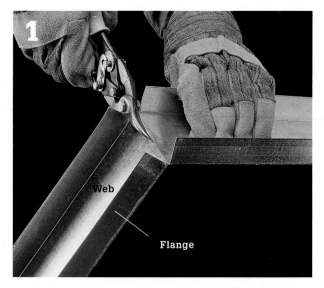

Mark the wall location on the floor or ceiling, following the same procedure used for a wood-frame wall. Cut the top and bottom tracks to length with aviation snips. Cut through the side flanges first, then bend the waste piece back and cut across the web. Use a marker to lay out the tracks with 16" on-center spacing.

Fasten the bottom track to the floor. For wood floors, use 2" coarse-thread drywall screws. For concrete floors, pin the track down with a powder-actuated nailer (see page 127), or use 1¼" masonry screw. Drill pilot holes for screws using a masonry bit. Drive a fastener at each end of the track, then every 24" in between.

Plumb up from the bottom track with a plumb bob to position the top track. Fasten the top track to the ceiling joists with 1⅝" drywall screws. Drive two screws at each joist location.

At the first stud location, measure between the tracks and cut a stud to length. Insert the stud into the tracks at a slight angle and twist into place. *Note: Cut all subsequent studs from the same end so the punch-outs align.*

Clamp the stud flange to the track with C-clamp pliers and drive a ⁷⁄₁₆" Type S panhead screw through the tracks into the stud. Drive one screw on each side at both ends of the stud. Install remaining studs so the open sides face the same direction (except at door-frame studs).

To install a door header, cut the track 8" longer than the opening. Measure in 4" at each end, cut the flanges at an angle toward the mark, then bend down the ends at 90°. Fasten the header in place with three screws at each stud—two through the fastening tab and one through the overlapping flange.

To provide running blocking for cabinets, wainscoting, or other fixtures, snap a chalk line across the face of the studs at the desired height, hold a track level at the line, then notch the flanges of the track to bypass the studs. Fasten the track in place with two screws at each stud location.

Building Materials Toxicity ▸

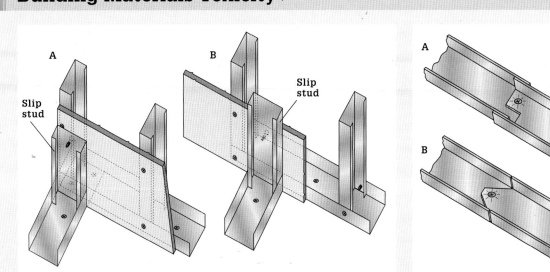

Build corners using a slip stud: A slip stud is not fastened until the adjacent drywall is in place. Form L-shaped corners (A) by overlapping the tracks. Cut off the flange on one side of one track, removing enough to allow room for the overlapping track and drywall. Form a T-shaped corner (B) by leaving a gap between the tracks for the drywall. Secure each slip stud by screwing through the stud into the tracks of the adjacent wall. Also screw through the back side of the drywall into the slip stud, if possible. Where there's no backing behind the slip stud, drive screws at a 45° angle through the back corners of the slip stud and into the drywall.

Join sections with a spliced joint (A) or notched joint (B). Make a spliced joint by cutting a 2" slit in the web of one track. Slip the other track into the slit and secure with a screw. For a notched joint cut back the flanges of one track and taper the web so it fits into the other track; secure with a screw.

Framing Soffits

Unfinished basements and other areas often contain elements like beams, pipes, and ductwork that may be vital to your house but become big obstacles to finishing the space. When you can't conceal the obstructions within walls, and you've determined it's too costly to move them, hide them inside a framed soffit or chase. This can also provide a place to run smaller mechanicals, like wiring and water supply lines.

You can frame a soffit with a variety of materials. 2 × 2 lumber and 1⅝" steel studs. Both work well including because they're small and lightweight (though steel is usually easier to work with because it's always straight). For large soffits that will house lighting fixtures or other elements, you might want the strength of 2 × 4s or three and ⅝" steel studs.

There may be code restrictions about the types of mechanicals that can be grouped together, as well as minimum clearances between the framing and what it encloses. Most codes also specify that soffits,

chases, and other framed structures have fireblocking every ten feet. and at the intersections between soffits and neighboring walls. Remember, too, that drain cleanouts and shutoff valves must be accessible, so you'll need to install access panels at these locations.

Soffits will require an access panel if they house electrical junction boxes or shutoff for water or gas supply lines. You can plan these into your framing or create them after the wallcovering is installed, as in the framed opening above. Here, a wood frame is glued to the soffit to create support ledges for the removable wallboard cutout.

A soffit is a bump-out that drops down from the ceiling to conceal ductwork, recessed light fixtures and other obstructions.

Variations for Building Soffits

2 × 2 soffit: Build two ladder-like frames for the soffit sides using standard 2 × 2s. Install braces every 16 or 24" to provide nailing support for the edges of the drywall. Attach the side frames to the joists on either side of the obstruction using nails or screws. Then, install crosspieces beneath the obstacle, tying the two sides together.

Simple steel-frame soffit: With ½" drywall, this construction works for soffits up to 16" wide; with ⅝" drywall, up to 24" wide. Use 1⅝, 2½, or 3⅝" steel studs and tracks (see pages 136 to 139). Fasten a track to the ceiling and a stud to the adjoining wall using drywall screws. Cut a strip of drywall to form the side of the soffit, and attach a steel stud flush with the bottom edge of the strip using Type S screws. Attach the assembly to the ceiling track, then cut and install drywall panels to form the soffit bottom.

Steel-frame soffit with braces: Use 1⅝, 2½, or 3⅝" steel studs and tracks. Fasten a track to the ceiling and wall with drywall screws. Cut studs to form the side and bottom of the soffit, fasten them to the tracks every 16 or 24" on-center, using Type S panhead screws, then join the pieces with metal angle (you can use a steel track cut in half lengthwise). Use a string line and locking clamps to help keep the frame straight and square during construction.

Installing Drywall

Drywall is inexpensive, perfectly uniform, and easy to install, making it the best choice for do-it-yourselfers working on remodeling projects. But there is a catch. In recent years, builders and homeowners have become aware of a limitation of drywall that has particular bearing on basements: black mold and mildew love drywall face paper, which can lead to serious air quality problems in damp basements. To combat this, manufacturers have developed drywall products that resist mold infestation. For basement remodeling, always choose mold-resistant panels.

If you are unable to locate any mold-resistant drywall, the next best choice is moisture-resistant drywall. Commonly called greenboard or blueboard, it is designed to withstand occasional contact with moisture. For areas that will receive tile, use a tile backer or cementboard.

Drywall comes in four-foot-wide panels in lengths ranging from eight to 16 feet and in thicknesses of ¼, ⅜, ½, and ⅝" (although your size choices currently are more limited with mold-resistant drywall). Standard half-inch panels are appropriate for walls and for ceilings with sixteen inch on-center framing. Where ceiling framing is 24 inches on-center, ⅝"-thick panels are recommended to prevent sagging.

Hanging wallboard is not a task many people look forward to, but compared to the mess and tediousness of finishing wallboard it isn't so bad.

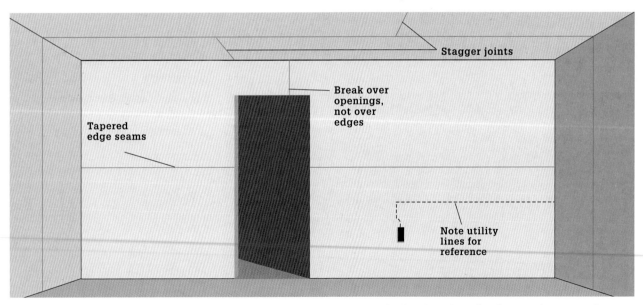

Stagger joints

Break over openings, not over edges

Tapered edge seams

Note utility lines for reference

Wallboard seams must fall on the centers of framing members, so measure the framing when planning your layout. Use long sheets to span an entire wall, or hang sheets vertically. Avoid butted end joints whenever possible; where they do occur, stagger them between rows so they don't fall on the same framing member. Don't place seams over the corners of doors, windows, and other openings: joints here often crack or cause bulges that interfere with trim. Where framing contains utility lines, draw a map for future reference noting locations of wiring, pipes, and shutoff valves.

Preparation Tips

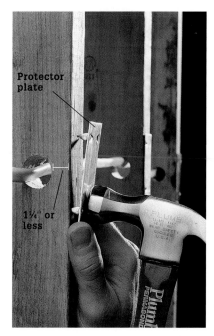

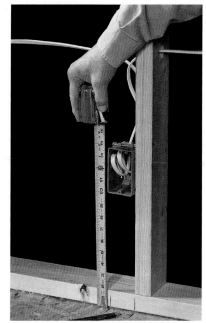

Install protector plates where wires or pipes pass through framing members and are less than 1¼" from the front edge. The plates keep drywall screws from puncturing wires or pipes.

Wrap cold-water pipes along the ceiling with foam insulation before covering them with drywall. This prevents condensation on the pipes that can drip onto the drywall and cause staining.

Mark the location and dimensions of electrical boxes on the floor. This makes it easier to locate them during wallboard installation.

Use a plane or chisel on studs that bow slightly. Trim the facing edge just enough so it is flush with the surrounding framing.

Studs in non-load-bearing walls bowed inward more than ¼" can be straightened. Using a handsaw, make a 2" cut into the stud at the midpoint of the bow. Pull the stud outward, and glue a tapered wood shim into the saw cut to hold the stud straight. Attach a 2-ft.-long 2 × 4 brace to one side of the stud to strengthen it, then trim off the shim. For studs that bow outward, plane down the stud surface with a portable power plane or hand plane. Replace any studs that are severely twisted.

How to Make Straight Wallboard Cuts

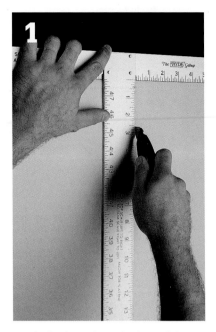

Mark the length on the face of the panel, then set a T-square at the mark. Hold the square in place with your hand and foot, and cut through the face paper using a utility knife with sharp blade.

Bend the scored section backward with both hands to snap the gypsum core.

Fold back the waste piece and cut through the back paper with the utility knife.

How to Cut Notches

Using a large drywall saw, cut the vertical sides of the notch. (These saws are also handy for cutting out door and window openings after the drywall is installed.)

Cut the face paper along the bottom of the notch using a utility knife. Snap the waste piece backward to break the core, then cut through the back paper.

How to Cut Large Openings

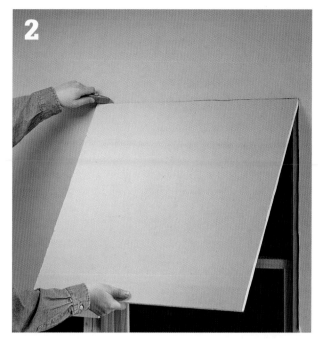

Measure the location of the cutout and transfer the dimensions to the backside of the panel. Score along the line that represents the header of the opening using a straightedge and utility knife.

Install the panel over the opening. The scored line should fall at the header. Cut the wallboard along the jambs and up to the header using a wallboard saw. Snap forward the waste piece to break the core, then cut through the face paper and remove.

How to Mark & Cut Electrical Box Openings

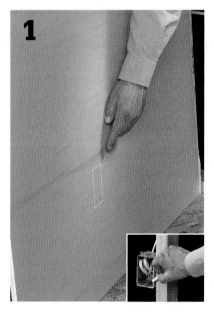

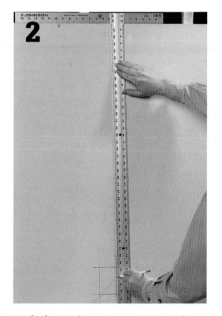

Use chalk or lipstick to rub the front edge of the electrical box (inset) and then position the wallboard panel and press it against the box to mark the opening.

Variation: Take measurements and plot out the coordinates onto the wallboard sheet.

Drill a pilot hole in one corner of the outline, then make the cutout with a key hole saw.

Hanging Wallboard

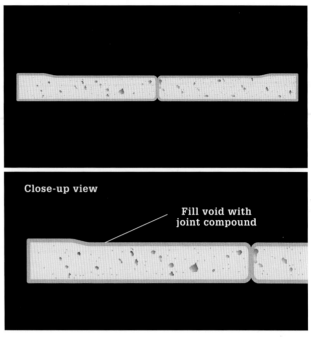

Where untapered panel ends will be butted together, bevel-cut the outside edges of each panel at 45°, removing about ⅛" of material. This helps prevent the paper from creating a ridge along the seam. Peel off any loose paper from the edge.

Close-up view

Fill void with joint compound

Butt tapered edges together wherever possible to create a shallow trough for joint compound and wallboard seam tape.

Adhesives create stronger bonds than fasteners, and reduce the number of screws needed for panel installation. Apply a ⅜" bead along framing members, stopping 6" from the panel edges (left). At butt joints, apply beads to both sides of the joint (right). Panels are then fastened along the perimeter.

At panel edges, drive fasteners ⅜" from the edges, making sure to hit the framing squarely. If the fastener tears the paper or crumbles the edge, drive another about 2" away from the first.

Recess all screws to provide a space, called a dimple, for the joint compound. However, driving a screw too far and breaking the paper renders it useless. If this happens, drive another screw about 2" away.

How to Hang Wallboard on Ceilings

1

2

Snap a chalk line perpendicular to the joists, 48⅛" from the starting wall.

Measure to make sure the first panel will break on the center of a joist. If necessary, cut the panel on the end that abuts the side wall so the panel breaks on the next farthest joist. Load the panel onto a rented drywall lift, or use a helper, and lift the panel flat against the joists.

3

4

Tip ▶

Position the panel with the leading edge on the chalk line and the end centered on a joist. Fasten the panel with 1¼" wallboard screws every 8" along edges and 12" in field (consult your local building department).

After the first row of panels is installed, begin the next row with a half-panel. This ensures that the butted end joints will be staggered between rows.

Drywall stilts bring you within reach of ceilings, so you can fasten and finish the drywall without a ladder. Stilts are commonly available at rental centers and are surprisingly easy to use.

How to Hang Wallboard on Walls

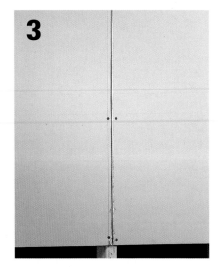

Measure from the wall end or corner to make sure the first panel will break on the center of the stud. If necessary, trim the sheet on the side or end that will be placed in the corner. Mark the stud centers on the panel face and pre-drive screws at each location along the top edge to facilitate fastening. Apply adhesive to the studs, if necessary.

With a helper or a wallboard lift, hoist the first panel tight against the ceiling, making sure the side edge is centered on a stud. Push the panel flat against the framing and drive the starter screws to secure the panel. Make any cutouts, then fasten the field of the panel.

Measure, cut, and install the remaining panels along the upper wall. Bevel panel ends slightly, leaving a ⅛" gap between them at the joint. Butt joints can also be installed using back blocking to create a recess.

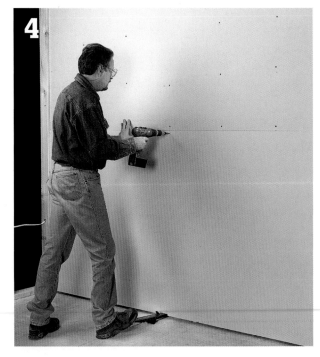

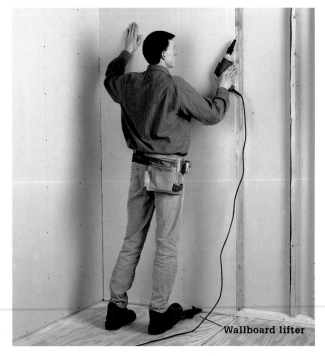

Wallboard lifter

Measure, cut, and install the bottom row, butting the panels tight to the upper row and leaving a ½" gap at the floor. Secure to the framing along the top edge using the starter screws, then make all cutouts before fastening the rest of the panel.

Variation: When installing wallboard vertically, cut each panel so it's ½" shorter than the ceiling height to allow for expansion. (The gap will be covered by base molding.) Avoid placing tapered edges at outside corners, which makes them difficult to finish.

Managing Corners

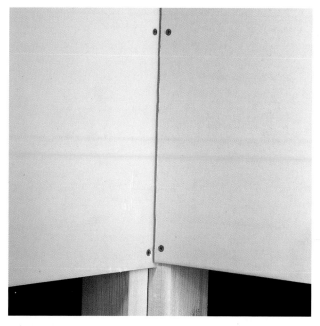

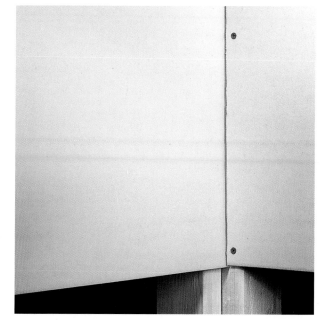

Standard 90° inside corners are installed with the first panel butted against the framing and the adjacent panel butted against the first. The screw spacing remains the same as on a flat wall.

Use a "floating corner" to reduce the chances of popped fasteners and cracks. Install the first panel, fastening only to within one stud bay of the corner. Push the leading edge of the adjacent panel against the first to support the unfastened edge. Fasten the second panel normally, including the corner.

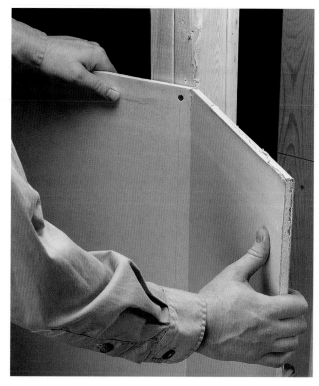

At outside corners, run panels long so they extend past the corner framing. Fasten the panel in place, then score the backside and snap cut to remove the waste piece.

For standard 90° outside corners, install the first panel so the outside edge is flush with the framing, then install the adjacent panel so it overlaps the end of the first panel.

Finishing Drywall

Finishing drywall is the more difficult phase of surfacing walls and ceilings, but it's a project well within the ability of any homeowner. Armed with a basic understanding of the variety of finish materials available, you'll be able to walk out of your local home center with the exact supplies you need to cover all joints, corners, and fasteners for a successful wallboard finish project.

Corner bead is the angle strip, usually made of metal or vinyl, that covers a wallboard corner, creating a straight, durable edge where walls intersect. Most corner beads are installed over the wallboard and are finished with compound. In addition to standard 90° outside-corner bead, there's an ever-growing variety of bead types designed for specific situations and easy application. There are beads for inside corners, flexible beads for off-angles and curves, J-beads and L-beads for flat panel edges, and bullnose beads for creating rounded inside and outside corners. While metal beads are installed with fasteners, vinyl beads can be installed with vinyl adhesive and staples, or be embedded in joint compound using the same techniques for installing paper-faced beads.

A selection of taping knives is required to handle different parts of the process of applying joint tape and compound. A 6" knife is used for the initial compound application of tape beds and to set tape into the beds. A 12" knife is used for the final coat, and a knife with an L-shaped blade gets into corners.

Joint tape is combined with joint compound to create a permanent layer that covers the wallboard seams, as well as small holes and gaps. Without tape, thick applications of compound are highly prone to cracking. There are two types of joint tape—paper and self-adhesive fiberglass mesh.

Joint compound, commonly called mud, seals and levels all seams, corners, and depressions in a wallboard installation. It's also used for skim-coating and some texturing treatments. There are several types of compounds with important differences among them, but the two main forms are setting-type and drying-type.

Setting-type compound is sold in dry powder form that is mixed with water before application. Because it dries through chemical reaction, setting compound dries quickly and is virtually unaffected by humidity and temperature. Setting compounds generally shrink less, bond better, and become harder than drying types, but they're more difficult to sand, a characteristic that makes them a better choice for the taping coat than for the filler and final coats. Drying-type compounds dry through evaporation and usually take about 24 hours to dry completely. Available in dry powder and convenient premixed forms in resealable one- and five-gallon buckets, drying compounds are highly workable and consistent.

Achieving a smooth wall surface depends completely on how well you manage the taping, "mudding," and sanding tasks in your project.

How to Install Metal Corner Bead

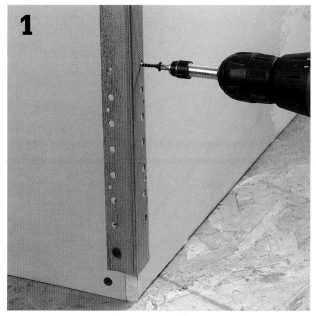

1

Starting at the top, fasten the bead flanges with 1¼"
drywall screws driven every 9" and about ¼" from the edge.
Alternate sides with each screw to keep the bead centered.
The screws must not project beyond the raised spine.

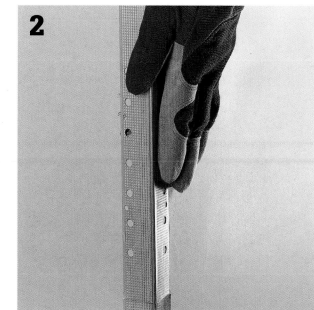

2

Use full lengths of corner bead where possible. If you must
join two lengths, cut the two pieces to size, then butt together
the finished ends. Make sure the ends are perfectly aligned
and the spine is straight along the length of the corner. File
ends, if necessary.

How to Install Vinyl Corner Bead

1

Cut vinyl bead to length and test fit over corner. Spray vinyl
adhesive evenly along the entire length of the corner, then
along the bead.

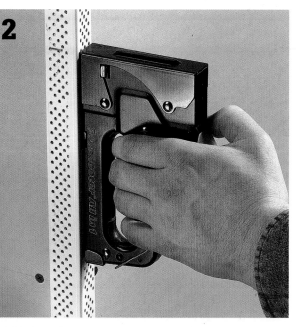

2

Quickly install the bead, pressing the flanges into the
adhesive. Fasten the bead in place with ½" staples every 8".

The Finishing Sequence ▶

Finishing newly installed drywall is satisfying work that requires patience and some basic skill, but it's easier than most people think. Beginners make their biggest, and most lasting, mistakes by rushing the job and applying too much compound in an attempt to eliminate coats. But even for professionals, drywall finishing involves three steps, and sometimes more, plus the final sanding. The first step is the taping coat, when you tape the seams between the drywall panels. If you're using standard metal corner bead on the outside corners, install it before starting the taping coat; paper-faced beads go on after the tape. The screw heads get covered with compound at the beginning of each coat. After the taping comes the second, or filler, coat. This is when you leave the most compound on the wall, filling in the majority of each depression. With the filler coat, the walls start to look pretty good, but they don't have to be perfect; the third coat will take care of minor imperfections. Lightly sand the second coat, then apply the final coat.

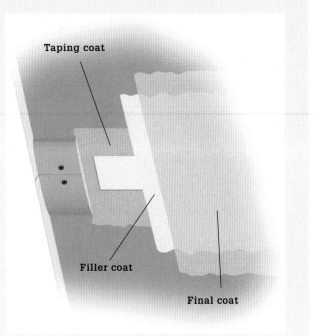

Taping coat

Filler coat

Final coat

How to Mix Joint Compound

Mix powdered setting-type compound with cool, potable water in a clean 5-gal. bucket, following the manufacturer's directions. All tools and materials must be clean—dirty water, old compound, and other contaminants will affect compound set time and quality.

Use a heavy-duty drill with a mixing paddle to thoroughly mix the compound to a stiff yet workable consistency. Use a low speed to avoid whipping air into the compound. Do not overwork setting-type compound, as it will begin setup. For powdered drying-type compound, remix after 15 minutes. Clean tools thoroughly immediately after use.

Use a hand masher to loosen premixed compound. If the compound has been around a while and is stiff, add a little water and mix to an even consistency.

How to Tape & Mud

1 Using a 4 or 6" taping knife, apply compound over each screw head, forcing it into the depression. Firmly drag the knife in the opposite direction, removing excess compound from the panel surface.

2 Apply an even bed layer of setting-type compound about ⅛" thick and 6" wide over tapered seams using a 6" taping knife. *Note: With paper tape, you can also use premixed taping or all-purpose compound.*

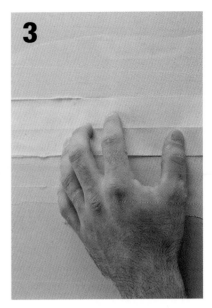

3 Center the tape over the seam and lightly embed it in the compound, making sure the tape is smooth and straight. At the end of the seam, tear off the tape so it extends all the way into the inside corners and up to the corner bead at outside corners.

4 Smooth the tape with the taping knife, working out from the center. Apply enough pressure to force compound from underneath the tape, so the tape is flat and has a thin layer beneath it.

5 At inside corners, smooth the final bit of tape by reversing the knife and carefully pushing it toward the corner. Carefully remove excess compound along the edges of the bed layer with the taping knife.

6 Cover vertical butt seams with a ⅛"-thick layer of joint compound. You should try and avoid this kind of joint, but in some cases there is no way around it. Cover the compound with seam tape and more compound. Make the taped area extrawide so you can feather it back gradually.

(continued)

7

Fold precreased paper tape in half to create a 90° angle to tape inside corners.

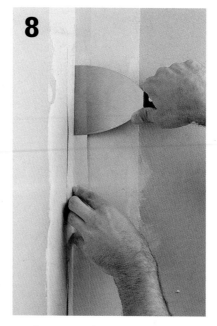

8

Apply an even layer of setting-type compound about ⅛" thick and 3" wide, to both sides of the corner, using a 4" taping knife. Embed the tape into the compound using your fingers and a taping knife.

9

Carefully smooth and flatten both sides of the tape, removing excess compound to leave only a thin layer beneath. Make sure the center of the tape is aligned straight with the corner.

Tip ▶

An inside corner knife can embed both sides of the tape in one pass—draw the knife along the tape, applying enough pressure to leave a thin layer of compound beneath. Feather each side using a straight 6" taping knife, if necessary.

10

Finish outside corner bead with a 6" knife. Apply the compound while dragging the knife along the raised spine of the bead. Make a second pass to feather the outside edge of the compound, then a third dragging along the bead again. Smooth any areas where the corner bead meets taped corners or seams.

11

Scrape off any remaining ridges and chunks after the taping coat has dried completely, then second-coat the screw heads, using a 6" taping knife and all-purpose compound. *Note: Setting-type compound and drying-type topping compound are also acceptable.*

12

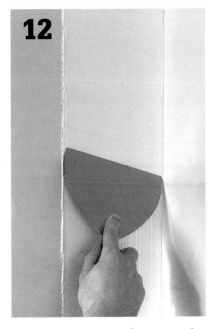

Apply an even layer of compound to both sides of each inside corner using a 6" taping knife. Smooth one side at a time, holding the blade about 15° from horizontal and lightly dragging the point along the corner. Make a second pass to remove excess compound along the outer edges. Repeat, if necessary.

13

Coat tapered seams with an even layer of all-purpose compound using a 12" taping knife. Whenever possible, apply the coat in one direction and smooth it in the opposite. Feather the sides of the compound first, holding the blade almost flat and applying pressure to the outside of the blade so the blade just skims over the center of the seam.

14

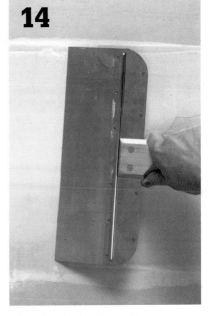

After feathering both side edges of the compound, make a pass down the center of the seam, applying even pressure to the blade. This pass should leave the seam smooth and even, with the edges feathered out to nothing. The joint tape should be completely covered.

15

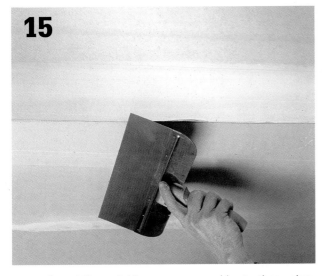

Second-coat the outside corners, one side at a time, using a 12" knife. Apply an even layer of compound, then feather the outside edge by applying pressure to the outside of the knife—enough so that the blade flexes and removes most of the compound along the edge but leaves the corner intact. Make a second pass with the blade riding along the raised spine, applying even pressure.

16

After the filler coat has dried, lightly sand all of the joints, then third-coat the screws. Apply the final coat, following the same steps used for the filler coat but do the seams first, then the outside corners, followed by the inside corners. Use a 12" knife and spread the compound a few inches wider than the joints in the filler coat. Remove most of the compound, filling scratches and low spots but leaving only traces elsewhere. Make several passes, if necessary, until the surface is smooth and there are no knife tracks or other imperfections. Carefully blend intersecting joints so there's no visible transition.

How to Sand Joint Compound

1

Use sheet plastic and 2" masking tape to help confine dust to the work area. Cover all doorways, cabinets, built-ins, and any gaps or other openings with plastic, sealing all four edges with tape, otherwise the fine dust produced by sanding can find its way through.

2

Knockdown any ridges, chunks or tool marks prior to sanding, using a 6" taping knife. Do not apply too much pressure—you don't want to dig into the compound, only remove the excess.

Tip ▶

As you work, if you oversand or discover low spots that require another coat of compound, mark the area with a piece of tape for repair after you finish sanding. Make sure to wipe away dust so the tape sticks to the surface.

3

Lightly sand all seams and outside corners using a pole sander with 220-grit sanding screen or 150-grit sandpaper. Work in the direction of the joints, applying even pressure to smooth transitions and high areas. Don't sand out depressions; fill them with compound and resand. Be careful not to over-sand or expose joint tape.

4

Inside corners often are finished with only one or two thin coats of compound over the tape. Sand the inside edge of joints only lightly and smooth the outside edge carefully; inside corners will be sanded by hand later.

5

Fine-sand the seams, outside corners, and fastener heads using a sanding block with 150- to 220-grit sanding screen or sandpaper. As you work, use your hand to feel for defects along the compound. A bright work light angled to highlight seams can help reveal problem areas.

6

To avoid damage from oversanding, use a 150-grit dry sanding sponge to sand inside corners. The sides of sanding sponges also contain grit, allowing you to sand both sides of a corner at once to help prevent oversanding.

7

For tight or hard-to-reach corners, fold a piece of sanding screen or sandpaper in thirds and sand the area carefully. Rather than using just your fingertips, try to flatten your hand as much as possible to spread out the pressure to avoid sanding too deep.

8

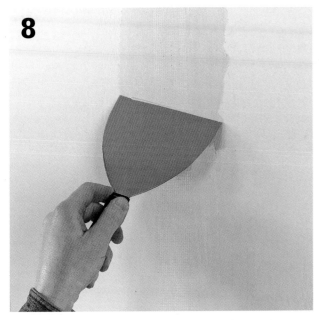

Repair depressions, scratches or exposed tape due to oversanding after final sanding is complete. Wipe the area with a dry cloth to remove dust, then apply a thin coat of all-purpose compound. Allow to dry thoroughly, then resand.

9

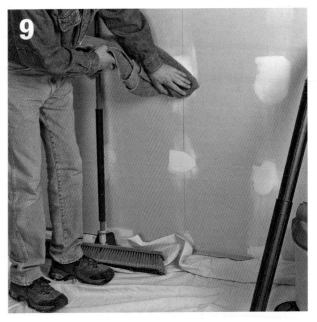

With sanding complete, remove dust from the panels with a dry towel or soft broom. Use a wet-dry vacuum to clean out all electrical boxes and around floors, windows, and doors, then carefully roll up sheet plastic and discard. Finally, damp mop the floor to remove any remaining dust.

Installing Paneling

Paneling is a versatile wall-surfacing material that comes in a wide range of styles, colors, and prices. Paneling sheets are made from a variety of materials for numerous applications, most of which are suitable for basement installations.

Laminate panels are sheets of MDF, particleboard, or plywood faced with paper, print, or vinyl. Laminates are available in hundreds of colors, styles, and patterns, providing a durable alternative to paint or wallcoverings. If you routinely have moisture problems in your basement, avoid these in favor of paneling that doesn't have a wood-based backing.

FRP (fiberglass reinforced plastic), extruded plastic, and vinyl panels contain solid material throughout the panel, creating a low-maintenance, water-resistant wall surface for bathrooms, utility rooms, garages, and workshops, as well as having numerous commercial applications.

Mark cutouts on back of paneling sheet by coloring the edges of electrical boxes with chalk or lipstick and then pressing the panel against the box.

Paneling is popular in basement rooms because it is inexpensive and doesn't require finishing. With the exception of solid PVC tileboard, most paneling is made from a base layer of hardboard or lauan plywood covered with a printed facing.

Tileboard is moisture-resistant hardboard coated with melamine, providing a durable, easy-to-clean plastic finish. It's designed to replicate the appearance of ceramic tile and is especially popular in bathrooms.

Most paneling is available in 4 × 8, 4 × 9, and 4 × 10 sheets. Some manufacturers also offer sheets in 60-inch widths. Paneling that is ¼" or less in thickness requires a solid backer of at least ½" wallboard; paneling ⅜" thick or more is rigid enough to be fastened directly to framing with 16-inch O.C. spacing. Installation typically involves a panel adhesive, either applied in beads along the wall or framing, or troweled onto the back surface of the panel. Make sure to check the manufacturer's instructions for the product you purchase.

To estimate the number of paneling sheets you'll need, measure the total width of the walls and divide by 48 inches. For every door subtract half a sheet, for every window, a quarter sheet.

Before installing paneling, condition it to the room it will be installed in for at least twenty-four hours. Stand sheets upright along their long edge, either separately or stacked together with wood spacers between each sheet to allow air to flow.

How to Install Paneling

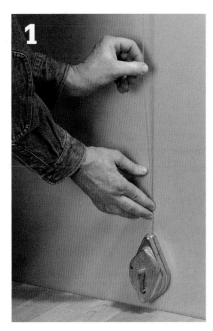

Starting in the corner farthest from the entry, use a stud finder to locate the center of the stud closest to, but less than, 48" from the corner. Find and mark stud centers every 48" from this first stud. Snap a plumb chalk line down the wall at each location. Paneling seams will fall along these lines.

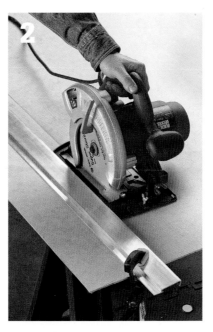

Lay the first paneling sheet face-side down. Measure the distance from corner to the first plumb mark and add 1" to allow for scribing. Use a circular saw and clamped straightedge to cut paneling to this measurement.

Apply stain or paint to the wall at the plumb lines so the backer will not show through the slight gaps at joints. Select a stain that matches the color of the paneling edges, which may be darker than the paneling surface.

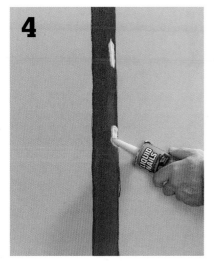

Use a caulk gun to apply 2"-long wavy beads of panel adhesive to the wall at 6" intervals about 1" back from plumb lines (to prevent adhesive from seeping out through the joints). For new construction, apply adhesive directly to the studs.

Attach the paneling to the top of the wall using 4d finishing nails driven every 16". Press the paneling against the adhesive, then pull it away from the wall. Press the paneling back against the wall when the adhesive is tacky, about 2 minutes.

Hang the remaining paneling so that there is a slight space at the joints. This space allows paneling to expand in damp weather. Use a dime as a spacing gauge.

Installing a Suspended Ceiling

Suspended ceilings are traditionally popular ceiling finishes for basements because they hang below pipes and other mechanicals, providing easy access to them. Suspended ceiling tile manufacturers have a wide array of ceiling tiles to choose from. Popular styles mimic historical tin tiles and add depth to the ceiling while minimizing sound and vibration noise.

A suspended ceiling is a grid framework made of lightweight metal brackets hung on wires attached to ceiling or floor joists. The frame consists of T-shaped main beams (mains), cross tees (tees), and L-shaped wall angles. The grid supports ceiling panels, which rest on the flanges of the framing pieces. Panels are available in 2 × 2-ft. or 2 × 4-ft., in a variety of styles. Special options include insulated panels, acoustical panels that absorb sound, and light-diffuser screens for use with fluorescent lights. Generally, metal-frame ceiling systems are more durable than ones made of plastic.

To begin your ceiling project, devise the panel layout based on the size of the room, placing equally sized trimmed panels on opposite sides to create a balanced look. Your ceiling must also be level.

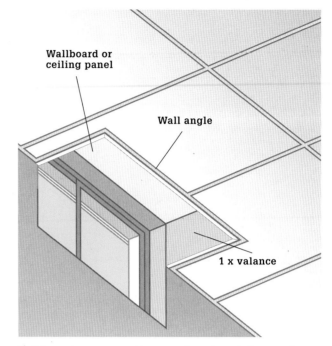

Build a valance around basement awning windows so they can be opened fully. Attach 1× lumber of an appropriate width to joists or blocking. Install drywall (or a suspended-ceiling panel trimmed to fit) to the joists inside the valance.

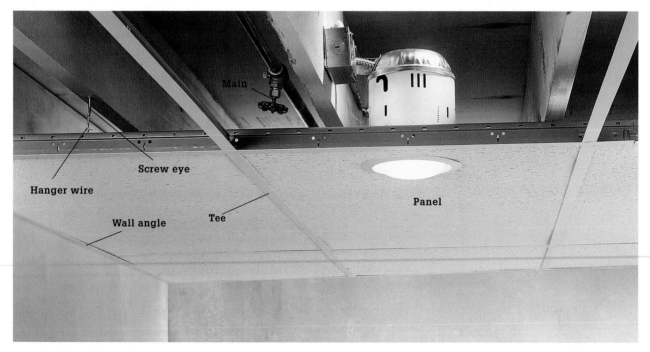

Suspended ceilings are very practical in basement rooms, and you can find them in many more design choices than you might expect.

How to Install a Suspended Ceiling

1

Make a mark on one wall that represents the ceiling height plus the height of the wall angle. Use a water level to transfer that height to both ends of each wall. Snap a chalk line to connect the marks. This line represents the top of the ceiling's wall angle.

2

Attach wall angle pieces to the studs on all walls, positioning the top of the wall angle flush with the chalk line. Use 1½" drywall screws (or short masonry nails driven into mortar joints on concrete block walls). Cut angle pieces using aviation snips.

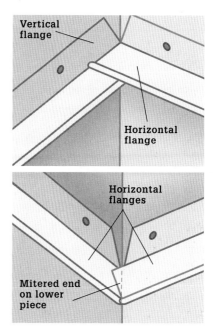

Vertical flange

Horizontal flange

Horizontal flanges

Mitered end on lower piece

Tip: Trim wall angle pieces to fit around corners. At inside corners (top), back-cut the vertical flanges slightly, then overlap the horizontal flanges. At outside corners (bottom), miter-cut one horizontal flange, and overlap the flanges.

3

Mark the location of each main on the wall angles at the ends of the room. The mains must be parallel to each other and perpendicular to the ceiling joists. Set up a guide string for each main using a thin string and lock-type clamps (inset). Clamp the strings to the opposing wall angles, stretching them very taut so there's no sagging.

4

Install screw eyes for hanging the mains using a drill and screw eye driver. Drill pilot holes and drive the eyes into the joists every 4 ft., locating them directly above the guide strings. Attach hanger wire to the screw eyes by threading one end through the eye and twisting the wire on itself at least three times. Trim excess wire, leaving a few inches of wire hanging below the level of the guide string.

(continued)

5

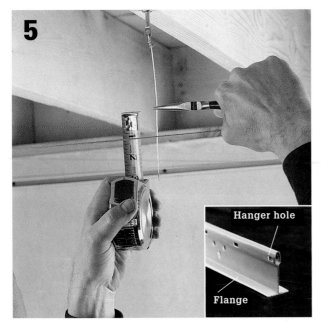

Hanger hole

Flange

Measure the distance from the bottom of a main's flange to the hanger hole in the web (inset). Use this measurement to prebend each hanger wire. Measure up from the guide string and make a 90° bend in the wire using pliers.

6

Following your ceiling plan, mark the placement of the first tee on opposite wall angles at one end of the room. Set up a guide string for the tee using a string and clamps, as before. This string must be perpendicular to the guide strings for the mains.

7

Tee slot

Trim one end of each main so that a tee slot in the main's web is aligned with the tee guide string, and the end of the main bears fully on a wall angle. Set the main in place to check the alignment of the tee slot with the string.

8

Cut the other end of each main to fit, so that it rests on the opposing wall angle. If a single main cannot span the room, splice two mains together end-to-end (the ends should be fashioned with male-female connectors). Make sure the tee slots remain aligned when splicing.

9

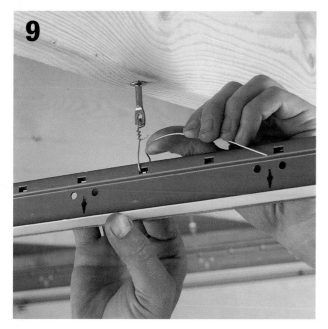

Install the mains by setting the ends on the wall angle and threading the hanger wires through the hanger holes in the webs. The wires should be as close to vertical as possible. Wrap each wire around itself three times, making sure the main's flange is level with the main guide string. Also install a hanger near each main splice.

10

Attach tees to the mains, slipping the tabbed ends into the tee slots on the mains. Align the first row of tees with the tee guide string; install the remaining rows at 4-ft. intervals. If you're using 2 × 2-ft. panels, install 2-ft. cross tees between the midpoints of the 4-ft. tees. Cut and install the border tees, setting the tee ends on the wall angles. Remove all guide strings and clamps.

11

Place full ceiling panels into the grid first, then install the border panels. Lift the panels in at an angle, and position them so they rest on the frame's flanges. Reach through adjacent openings to adjust the panels, if necessary.

12

To trim the border panels to size, cut them face-up using a straightedge and utility knife.

Installing an Acoustic Tile Ceiling

Easy-to-install ceiling tile can lend character to a plain ceiling or help turn an unfinished basement or attic into beautiful living space. Made of pressed mineral and fiberboard, ceiling tiles are available in a variety of styles. They also provide moderate noise reduction.

Ceiling tiles typically can be attached directly to a drywall or plaster ceiling with adhesive. If your ceiling is damaged or uneven, or if you have an unfinished joist ceiling, install 1 × 2 furring strips as a base for the tiles, as shown in this project. Some systems include metal tracks for clip-on installation.

Unless your ceiling measures in even feet, you won't be able to install the 12-inch tiles without some cutting. To prevent an unattractive installation with small, irregular tiles along two sides, include a course of border tiles along the perimeter of the installation. Plan so that tiles at opposite ends of the room are cut to the same width and are at least half the width of a full tile.

Most ceiling tile comes prefinished, but it can be painted to match any decor. For best results, apply two coats of paint using a roller with a ¼" nap, and wait 24 hours between coats.

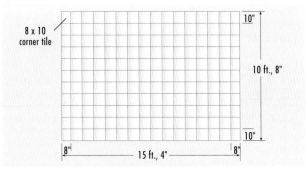

Measure the ceiling and devise a layout. If the length (or width) doesn't measure in even feet, use this formula to determine the width of the border tiles: add 12 to the number of inches remaining and divide by 2. The result is the width of the border tile. (For example, if the room length is 15 ft., 4", add 12 to the 4, then divide 16 by 2, which results in an 8" border tile.)

Acoustic tiles are attached to wood strips on the ceiling rather than suspended. They do not lower the ceiling height as much as a suspended ceiling, but they are also harder to remove for joist cavity access.

How to Install an Acoustic Tile Ceiling

Install the first furring strip flush with the wall and perpendicular to the joists, fastening with two 8d nails or 2" screws at each joist. Measure out from the wall a distance equal to the border tile width minus ¾" and snap a chalk line. Install the second furring strip with its wall-side edge on the chalk line.

Install the remaining strips 12" on-center from the second strip. Measure from the second strip and mark the joist nearest the wall every 12". Repeat along the joist on the opposite side of the room, then snap chalk lines between the marks. Install the furring strips along the lines. Install the last furring strip flush against the opposite side wall.

Check the strips with a 4-ft. level. Insert wood shims between the strips and joists as necessary to bring the strips into a level plane.

Cut border tiles with a utility knife to fit (inset). Position the corner tile with the flange edges aligned with the two string lines and fasten it to the furring strips with four ½" staples. Cut and install two border tiles along each wall, making sure the tiles fit snugly together.

Fill in between the border tiles with full-size tiles. Continue working diagonally in this manner toward the opposite corner. For the border tiles along the far wall, trim off the flange edges and staple through the faces of the tiles close to the wall.

Windows, Doors & Trim

Installing windows in exterior basement walls can be a good deal more complicated than putting them into the house walls. Not only do you have to drive fasteners into concrete instead of wood, if you need to enlarge an opening (a common requirement) there is no way of getting around cutting concrete. The most common basement window project is adding an egress window. Required in bedrooms and a good idea in any room, an egress window must meet specific size requirements that ensure it is big enough for an adult to escape through in an emergency.

Once the window opening is framed in wood, the installation is pretty much the same as anywhere else in your house. The same is true for interior doors and trim. If you have ever installed any of these items upstairs, you will have no problem doing the same in the basement.

In this chapter:

- Installing an Egress Window
- Replacing Basement Windows
- Trimming Basement Windows
- Installing Prehung Interior Doors
- Installing Pocket Doors
- Installing Bifold Doors
- Installing Walkout Patio Doors
- Installing Molding

Installing an Egress Window

An egress window brings a pleasant source of natural light and ventilation to a dark, dank basement. More importantly, it can provide a lifesaving means of escape in the event of a fire. Before you proceed with this project, read more about building code issues regarding basement egress on page 21. Contact your local building department to apply for the proper permits and to learn more about the code requirements for your area.

As long as the window opens wide enough to meet minimum standards for egress, the particular window style is really up to you. Casement windows are ideal, because they crank open quickly and provide unobstructed escape. A tall, double-hung window or wide sliding window can also work. Select a window with insulated glass and clad with vinyl or aluminum for durability; it will be subject to humidity and temperature fluctuations just like any other above-grade window in your home.

The second fundamental component of a basement egress window project is the subterranean escape well you install outside the foundation. There are several options to choose from: prefabricated well kits made of lightweight plastic that bolt together and are easy to install; corrugated metal wells that are a lower-cost option; or, a well built from scratch using concrete, stone, or landscape timber.

Installing an egress window involves four major steps: digging the well, cutting a new or larger window opening in the foundation, installing the window, and, finally, installing the well. You'll save time and effort if you hire a backhoe operator to excavate the well. In most cases, you'll also need a large concrete saw (available at most rental stores) to cut the foundation wall.

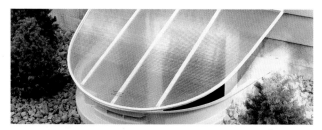

Replacing a small basement window with an egress window is a big job, but it is required if you want to convert part of a basement into livable space, especially a bedroom.

Tools & Materials ▸

Tape measure	Gloves
4-ft. level	Window well and
Stakes and string	window
line	Pea gravel
Shovel	Plastic sheeting
Colored masking	Self-tapping
tape	masonry screws
Hammer drill with	2× pressure-treated
½" dia. × 12- to	lumber
16"-long masonry	Shims
bit	Insulation materials
Masonry saw	Concrete sleeve
Hand maul	anchors
Cold chisel	Quick-curing
Trowel	concrete
Miter saw	3½" deck screws
Hammer	Foam backer rod
Drill/driver, hammer	Tamper
Caulk and caulk gun	

How to Install an Egress Window & Window Well

Lay out the border of the window well area with stakes and string. Plan the length and width of the excavation to be several feet larger than the window well's overall size to provide extra room for installation and adjustment.

Excavate the well to a depth 6 to 12" deeper than the well's overall height to allow room for drainage gravel. Make sure to have your local public utilities company inspect the well excavation area and okay it for digging before you start.

Measure and mark the foundation wall with brightly colored masking tape to establish the overall size of the window's rough opening (here, we're replacing an existing window). Be sure to take into account the window's rough opening dimensions, the thickness of the rough framing (usually 2x stock), and the width of the structural header you may need to build. Remember also that sill height must be within 44" of the floor. Remove existing wall coverings inside the layout area.

If the floor joists run perpendicular to your project wall, build a temporary support wall parallel to the foundation wall and 6 to 8 ft. from it. Staple sheet plastic to the wall and floor joists to form a work tent that will help control concrete dust.

(continued)

5

Drill reference holes at each bottom corner with a hammer drill and long masonry bit. These holes will provide reference points for cutting from both sides, ensuring clean breaks.

6

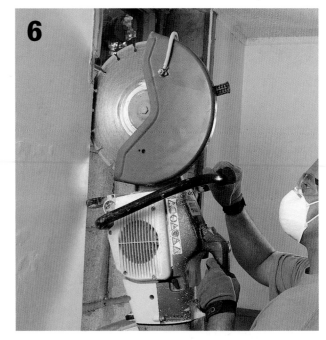

Equip a masonry cutting saw (or large angle grinder) with a diamond blade and set it for a ½" cut to score the blocks first. Then reset the saw to full depth and make the final bottom and side cuts through the blocks. Wear a tight-fitting particle mask, ear and eye protection, and gloves for all of this cutting work; the saw will generate a tremendous amount of thick dust. Feed the saw slowly and steadily. Stop and rest periodically so the dust can settle.

7

On the outside foundation wall, score the cuts, then make full-depth cuts.

8

Strike the blocks with a hand maul to break or loosen the block sections. When all the blocks are removed, carefully chip away remaining debris with a cold chisel to create flat surfaces.

9

Fill the hollow voids in concrete block walls, with broken pieces of block, then level and smooth the voids by trowelling on a fresh layer of quick-curing concrete. Flatten the surfaces, and allow the concrete to dry overnight.

10

If your project requires a new header above the new window, build it from pieces of 2× lumber sandwiching ½" plywood and fastened together with construction adhesive and 10d nails. Slip it into place and tack it temporarily to the mudsill with 3½" deck screws driven toenail style.

11

Cut the sill plate for the window's rough frame from 2× treated lumber that's the same width as the thickness of the foundation wall. Fasten the sill to the foundation with ³⁄₁₆ × 3¼" countersunk masonry screws. Drill pilot holes for the screws first with a hammer drill.

12

Cut two pieces of treated lumber just slightly longer than the opening so they'll fit tightly between the new header and sill. Tap them into place with a maul. Adjust them for plumb and fasten them to the foundation with countersunk masonry screws or powder-actuated fasteners.

(continued)

13

Apply a thick bead of silicone caulk around the outside edges of the rough frame and set the window in its opening, seating the nailing flanges into the caulk. Shim the window so the frame is level and plumb. Test the action of the window to make sure the shims aren't bowing the frame.

14

Attach the window's nailing flanges to the rough frame with screws or nails, as specified by the manufacturer. Check the window action periodically as you fasten it to ensure that it still operates smoothly.

15

Seal gaps between the rough frame and the foundation with a bead of exterior silicone or polyurethane caulk. If the gaps are wider than 1/4", insert a piece of backer rod first, then cover it with caulk. On the interior, fill gaps around the window shims with strips of foam backer rod, fiberglass insulation, or a bead of minimally expanding spray foam. Do not distort the window frame.

16

Fill the well excavation with 6 to 12" of pea gravel. This will serve as the window's drain system. Follow the egress well kit instructions to determine the exact depth required; you may need to add more gravel so the top of the well will be above the new window. *Note: We added a drain down to the foundation's perimeter tile for improved drainage as well.*

17

Set the bottom section of the well into the hole, and position it evenly from left to right relative to the window. Adjust the gravel surface to level the well section carefully.

18

Stack the second well section on top of the first, and connect the two with the appropriate fasteners.

19

Fasten the window well sections to the foundation wall with concrete sleeve anchors driven into prebored pilot holes. You could also use masonry nails driven with a powder-actuated tool.

20

When all the well sections are assembled and secured, nail pieces of trim around the window frame to hide the nailing flange. Complete the well installation by using excavated dirt to backfill around the outside of the well. Pack the soil with a tamper, creating a slope for good drainage. If you are installing a window well cover, set it in place and fasten it according to the manufacturer's instructions. The cover must be removable.

Replacing Basement Windows

Replacing an old and underperforming basement window can accomplish much in conjunction with your basement remodeling project. Newer windows can allow more light in while keeping drafts out. They may have ventilation capabilities that older fixed widows lack. They can offer better security, especially if you install a glass block window that does not let people see inside but still allows light into the room.

Most home centers sell basement windows in standard 32-inch wide sizes (standard heights are 13, 15, 17, 19 and 23 inches). The main types are awning windows that are hinged on top, hopper windows that are hinged on the bottom, and fixed windows. Some glass block or acrylic block fixed windows include a ventilation opening in lieu of one of the blocks.

If your basement window opening is not a standard size, you have three options. You can have a window custom-made (not as expensive as it sounds), you can remove the old window and enlarge the opening, or you can shrink the opening by using thicker lumber for the rough frame.

Basement windows are the only source of natural light, but they also can allow cold air or even intruders to enter. If you are remodeling your basement, it makes sense to update old windows with new ones that offer better energy efficiency and security.

How to Replace a Basement Window

Remove the old window and inspect the rough frame. If it shows signs of rot, remove the frame by cutting the sill and header in half and prying the halves out. Cut new frame members from pressure-treated dimension lumber.

Install the new rough frame using a powder-actuated tool to drive masonry nails. Apply several thick beads of caulk to the concrete surfaces first to create a good seal. The header and sill should run the full width of the opening and be installed before the side members. Caulk around the frame edges and paint the frame with exterior primer.

3

Position the new window unit in the opening and test it with a level. Use shims to raise it so it is not resting on the sill. Adjust it so the gaps are even on the sides. *Tip: You may find it easier to adjust and install the window frame if you remove the glass sash first.*

4

Attach the window frame to the rough frame opening with screws driven through the jambs. Often, the screw is access through a hole in the inner jamb layer. Arrange shims so the screws will pass through them. Do not overdrive screws—it can pull the window frame out of square.

5

Fill gaps between the rough window frame and the new window unit with minimal expanding spray foam. Do not spray in too much—it can distort the frame when it dries.

6

Install stop molding on both sides of the window to cover gaps between the window and the rough frame. Paint the stop molding and frame to match your trim color.

Trimming Basement Windows

Basement windows bring much-needed sunlight into dark areas, but even in finished basements they often get ignored on the trim front. This is partly because most basement foundation walls are at least eight inches thick, and often a lot thicker. Add a furred-out wall and the window starts to look more like a tunnel with a pane of glass at the end. But with some well-designed and well-executed trim carpentry, you can turn the depth disadvantage into a positive.

A basement window opening may be finished with wallboard, but the easiest way to trim one is by making extrawide custom jambs that extend from the inside face of the window frame to the interior wall surface. Because of the extra width, plywood stock is a good choice for the custom jambs. The project shown here is created with veneer-core plywood with oak veneer surface. The jamb members are fastened together into a nice square frame using rabbet joints at the corner. The frame is scribed and installed as a single unit and then trimmed out with oak casing. The casing

is applied flush with the inside edges of the frame opening. If you prefer to have a reveal edge around the interior edge of the casing, you will need to add a solid hardwood strip to the edge of the frame so the plies of the plywood are not visible.

Tools & Materials ▸

Pencil	Finish-grade ¾" oak
Tape measure	plywood
Table saw	Spray-foam insulation
Drill with bits	1¼" composite or
2-ft. level	cedar wood shims
Framing square	2" finish nails
Utility knife	1⅝" drywall screws
Straightedge	Carpenter's glue

Because they are set into thick foundation walls, basement windows present a bit of a trimming challenge. But the thickness of the foundation wall also lets you create a handy ledge that's deep enough to hold potted plants or even sunning cats.

How to Trim a Basement Window

Check to make sure the window frame and surrounding area are dry and free of rot, mold, or damage. At all four corners of the basement window, measure from the inside edges of the window frame to the wall surface. Add 1" to the longest of these measurements.

Set your table saw to make a rip cut to the width arrived at in step 1. If you don't have a table saw, set up a circular saw and straightedge cutting guide to cut strips to this length. With a fine-tooth panel-cutting blade, rip enough plywood strips to make the four jamb frame components.

Miter gauge

Crosscut the plywood strips to correct lengths. In our case, we designed the jamb frame to be the exact same outside dimensions as the window frame, since there was some space between the jamb frame and the rough opening.

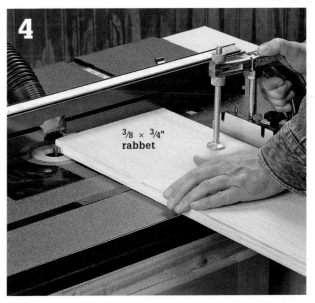

3/8 × 3/4" rabbet

Cut $\frac{3}{8}$"-deep × $\frac{3}{4}$"-wide rabbets at each end of the head jamb and the sill jamb. A router table is the best tool for this job, but you may use a table saw or handsaws and chisels. Inspect the jambs first and cut the rabbets in whichever face is in better condition. To ensure uniformity, we ganged the two jambs together (they're the same length). It's also a good idea to include backer boards to prevent tearout.

(continued)

Glue and clamp the frame parts together, making sure to clamp near each end from both directions. Set a carpenter's square inside the frame and check it to make sure it's square.

Before the glue sets, carefully drill three perpendicular pilot holes, countersunk, through the rabbeted workpieces and into the side jambs at each corner. Space the pilot holes evenly, keeping the end ones at least ¾" in from the end. Drive a 1⅝" drywall screw into each pilot hole, taking care not to overdrive. Double-check each corner for square as you work, adjusting the clamps if needed.

Let the glue dry for at least one hour (overnight is better), then remove the clamps and set the frame in the window opening. Adjust and shim the frame so it is centered and level in the opening and the exterior-side edges fit flush against the window frame.

Taking care not to disturb the frame's position (rest a heavy tool on the sill to hold it in place if you wish), press a straight edge against the wall surface and mark trimming points at the point where the rule meets the jambs at each side of all four frame corners using a sharp pencil.

Scribe line

Remove the frame and clamp it on a flat work surface. Use a straightedge to connect the scribe marks at the ends of each jamb frame side. Set the cutting depth of your circular saw to just a small fraction over ¾". Clamp a straightedge guide to the frame so the saw blade will follow the cutting line and trim each frame side in succession. (The advantage of using a circular saw here is that any tearout from the blade will be on the nonvisible faces of the frame.)

Replace the frame in the window opening in the same orientation as when you scribed it and install shims until it is level and centered in the opening. Drive a few finish nails through the side jambs into the rough frame. Also drive a few nails through the sill jamb. Most trim carpenters do not drive nails into the head jamb.

Insulate between the jamb frame and the rough frame with spray-in polyurethane foam. Look for minimal-expanding foam labeled "window and door" and don't spray in too much. Let the foam dry for a half hour or so and then trim off the excess with a utility knife. *Tip: Protect the wood surfaces near the edges with wide strips of masking tape.*

Remove the masking tape and clean up the mess from the foam (there is always some). Install case molding. We used picture-frame techniques to install fairly simple oak casing.

Installing Prehung Interior Doors

Install prehung interior doors after the framing work is complete and the wallboard has been installed. If the rough opening for the door has been framed accurately, installing the door takes about an hour.

Standard prehung doors have 4½"-wide jambs and are sized to fit walls with 2 × 4 construction and half-inch wallboard. If you have 2 × 6 construction or thicker wall surface material, you can special order a door to match, or you can add jamb extensions to a standard-sized door (see Tip, page 182).

One drawback to prehung doors is that they frequently are hollow-core doors, which means that they consist mostly of a couple of thin layers of veneer that sandwich a network of cardboard spacers. This is not necessarily a problem except when you need to shorten the door—a common situation in basements.

Prehung interior doors are a good choice for basements because they're fast to install and usually rather inexpensive.

How to Shorten a Hollowcore Door

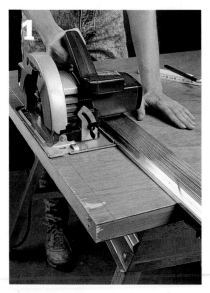

Draw a straight cutting line at the bottom of the door, not the top. Score along the line with a utility knife and then cut along the line with a circular saw and straightedge guide.

Strip the veneer from the frame rail with a chisel. If you cut through the frame and the top of the door still contains a frame, test it to see how sturdy it is. If there is more than ½" of rail still in the door you can go ahead and rehang the door in the frame.

Apply wood glue to the frame rail once the veneer is removed and insert the rail into the top of the hollow door. Adjust so the rail is flush along the top and let the glue dry before rehanging the door in the jambs (which you will also need to trim).

How to Install a Prehung Door

1

Unpack your door and remove any braces that are stapled to the jamb to keep the door from swinging in the jamb during transit.

2

Set the door in the framed opening with the door closed. Shift it so it is centered side to side and the jambs are flush with the wall surface. Check for plumb by placing a level on the hinge-side jamb. Shim as necessary and then open the door—the pressure from the shims should hold the door in place.

3

Anchor the hinge-side jamb with 8d casing nails driven through the jamb and shims and into the rough frame. If the jambs are made of hardwood such as oak, drill pilot holes for the nails.

4

Drive nails near the bottom hinge and then the middle, if your door has three hinges. Make sure to drive through shims. If you drive nails away from the shims the jambs may bow outward.

(continued)

5

Double-check the jamb on the strike plate side to make sure it is plumb and flush with the wall surface, and then nail it to the framing, nailing through the shims as you did on the hinge jamb.

6

Drive a few nails through pilot holes in the center of the door stop for reinforcement. Locate the nails so they go through shims.

Jamb Extensions ▶

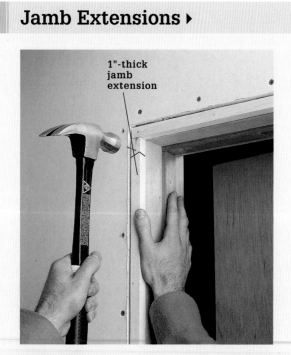

1"-thick jamb extension

If your walls are built with 2 × 6 studs, you'll need to extend the jambs by attaching 1"-thick wood strips to the edges of the jamb after the door is installed. Use glue and 4d casing nails when attaching jamb extensions. Make the strips from the same wood as the jamb.

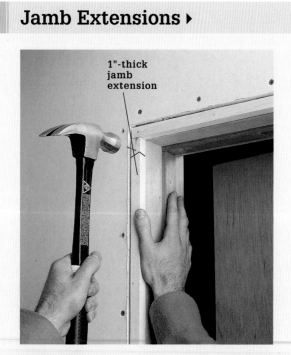

7

Attach the preattached case moldings to the framing members with 4d finish nails. Set the nail heads. Fill all nail holes with wood putty and then paint or stain. Use a nail set to recess the nail heads. Install a latch set (see next page).

How to Install a Latch Set

Knob

Mounting plate

Rosette

Screw post

Latch bolt

Spindle

Latch plate

Strike plate

A latch set is an interior doorknob set with a latch and strike plate. It is installed in doors that are not intended to be locked. A latch set with a locking mechanism is called a lockset.

Insert the latch bolt and latch plate assembly into the hole drilled in the edge of the door and fasten the plate to the door. Make sure the curved side of the end of the latch bolt is facing toward the door. The door edge usually is premortised so the plate is flush. If it is not, you'll need to cut a shallow mortise for the plate with a wood chisel.

Insert the spindle attached to one of the knobs through the same-shaped hole in the latch bolt. Hold the knob against the door and slide the other knob in place so the spindle fits into the spindle hole in the second knob.

Insert the long post screws into the screw opening and thread them into the screw holes in the opposite knob. Tighten them to draw the two halves of the knob set together. Do not overtighten.

Position the strike plate in the mortise in the jamb (cut one with a chisel if your jamb has no mortise). Make sure the latch bolt and the hole in the strike plate are aligned. Attach the strike plate to the jamb with the screw provided by the manufacturer.

Installing Pocket Doors

Pocket doors are a space-saving alternative to traditional hinged interior doors. Swinging doors can monopolize up to 16 square feet of floor space in a room, which is why pocket doors are a perfect choice for tight spaces, like small bathrooms. Installed in pairs, pocket doors can divide large rooms into more intimate spaces and can still be opened to use the entire area.

Pocket door hardware kits generally are universal and can be adapted for almost any interior door. In this project, the frame kit includes an adjustable track, steel-clad split studs, and all the required hanging hardware. The latch hardware, jambs, and the door itself are all sold separately. Pocket door frames can also be purchased as preassembled units that can be easily installed into a rough opening.

Framing and installing a pocket door is not difficult in new construction or a major remodel. But retrofitting a pocket door in place of a standard door or installing one in a wall without an existing door, is a major project that involves removing the wall material, framing the new opening, installing and hanging the door, and refinishing the wall. Hidden utilities, such as wiring, plumbing, and heating ducts, must be rerouted if encountered.

The rough opening for a pocket door is at least twice the width of a standard door opening. If the wall is load bearing, you will need to install an appropriately sized header.

Because pocket doors are easy to open and close and require no threshold, they offer increased accessibility for wheelchair or walker users, provided the handles are easy to use. If you are installing a pocket door for this purpose, be aware that standard latch hardware may be difficult to use for some individuals.

Tools & Materials ▸

Tape measure
Hammer
Nail set
Screwdriver
Level
Drill
Hacksaw
Wallboard tools
2 × 4 lumber
8d, and 6d common nails
Chalk line
Pocket door frame kit
Door
1¼" wallboard screws
Wallboard materials
Manufactured pocket door
    jambs (or cut jambs
    from 1× lumber)
8d and 6d finish nails
1½" wood screws
Door casing
Wood finishing materials

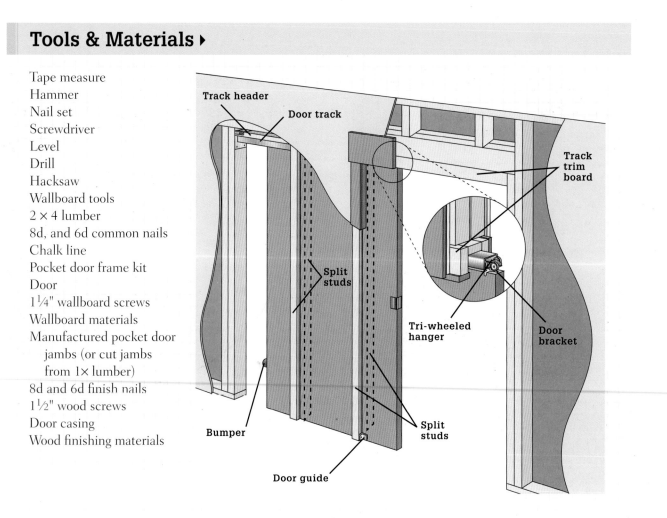

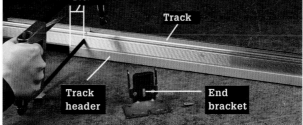

Frame the rough opening for the pocket door according to the manufacturer's sizing instructions. Determine the proper height for the overhead track and drive a nail at each side of the door opening. Leave the nailheads protruding slightly so you can support the track on them temporarily.

Cut the overhead track to length according to the width of the pocket door. The wooden portion of the track should be premarked with cutting lines for standard door sizes (top). The metal part of the track is cut shorter than the wood part (here, by 1⅜"). Attach the end brackets to the track after the trim cuts are made.

Position the overhead track in the framed opening, resting the end bracket on the nails driven in step 1 for temporary support. Center the assembly and secure it by driving 8d common nails through the nailing holes in the brackets.

Attach the split studs in the framed opening. Split studs are the secret to pocket doors. They have an open center that allows the door to pass through. Because they are reinforced with steel they can perform structural bearing comparable to a solid wood stud. Nail the split studs to the wooden part of the overhead track.

Fasten split studs to the floor by nailing through the bottom plate into the subfloor. Snap chalk lines aligned with the front and back of the sole plate in the framed opening as guidance.

(continued)

6

Fasten rolling brackets to the top of the door following the spacing recommended by the door manufacturer (usually a couple of inches in from each end). Attach wall coverings around the framed opening, making sure your fasteners are not long enough to protrude into the pocket. *Tip: Paint or stain the door before hanging it.*

7

Tri-wheeled hanger

Lock arm

Hang the door by pressing the bracket up into the tri-wheeled hangers in the overhead track and then snapping the lock arm over the hanger. If you have not installed floor covering yet, do so before proceeding to the trim installation.

8

Attach a full-width door jamb for the door to close against. Nail the jamb to the framed opening stud with 8d casing nails.

9

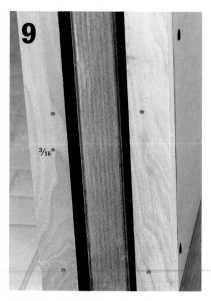

3/16"

Attach split jambs to the side of the framed opening housing the door. Maintain a gap of 3/16" between the door and the inside edges of the split jambs.

10

Install split head jambs with countersunk wood screws. This allows you to easily remove the head jamb if the door needs to be replaced or removed for repair.

11

Attach the latch and pull hardware, which is usually supplied with the door. Also attach door guide hardware at the wall opening to help track the door. Fill nail holes and finish the jambs and walls.

Installing Bifold Doors

Bifold doors provide easy access to a closet without requiring much clearance for opening. Most home centers stock kits that include two pairs of prehinged doors, a head track, and all the necessary hardware and fasteners. Typically, the doors in these kits have predrilled holes for the pivot and guide posts. Hardware kits are also sold separately for custom projects. There are many types of bifold door styles, so be sure to read and follow the manufacturer's instructions for the product you use.

Tools & Materials ▸

Tape measure	Hacksaw
Level	Prehinged bifold
Circular saw	doors
Straightedge	Head track
(optional)	Mounting hardware
Drill	Panhead screws
Plane	Flathead screws
Screwdriver	

How to Install Bifold Doors

Cut the head track to the width of the opening using a hacksaw. Insert the roller mounts into the track, then position the track in the opening. Fasten it to the header using panhead screws.

Measure and mark each side jamb at the floor for the anchor bracket so the center of the bracket aligns exactly with the center of the head track. Fasten the brackets in place with flathead screws.

Check the height of the doors in the opening, and trim if necessary. Insert pivot posts into predrilled holes at the bottoms and tops of the doors. Insert guide posts at the tops of the leading doors. Make sure all posts fit snugly.

Fold one pair of doors closed and lift into position, inserting the pivot and guide posts into the head track. Slip the bottom pivot post into the anchor bracket. Repeat for the other pair of doors. Close the doors and check alignment along the side jambs and down the center. If necessary, adjust the top and bottom pivots following the manufacturer's instructions.

Installing Walkout Patio Doors

A walkout basement without a patio door seems incomplete. Yet many homes with direct access into the basement do not take full advantage of the feature. A sliding or swingout patio door allows several times the amount of natural light into a room that a single door lets in, even if the single door has a large bright panel. If there is a patio or deck on the exterior side of your basement door, enlarging the door will make moving guests and supplies through the doorway much easier and more comfortable.

When choosing a new patio door, you'll need to decide between models with hinged doors that swing out and close together or ones with sliding door panels. Swinging doors tend to require less maintenance than sliding doors, and they offer better security. Sliding doors are a good choice if ventilation is one of your requirements, because the amount of air they let in is easy to regulate. You can also leave a sliding door open without the wind catching it and causing it to slam or break.

Enlarging a door opening requires that you make structural changes to your house, so it almost always requires a building permit. During construction you will need to provide temporary support to replace the bearing being done by the wall studs you'll need to cut. And when you install the new door, the framed opening must have a substantial header. Check with your local building department for the header requirements. Because basement ceilings may be shorter than eight feet, you may need to use a header that's fabricated from engineered beams to meet the load bearing requirements within the available space.

Tools & Materials ▸

Circular saw
Reciprocating saw
   with bi-metal
   blade
Handsaw
10d, 16d nails
2½" deck screws
½" plywood

Self-adhesive rubber
   flashing
Building paper
Drip edge molding
Panel adhesive
Fiberglass insulation
Case molding

BEFORE **AFTER**

Replacing a single door with a sliding patio door is a great way to add light to a walkout basement and create an inviting entryway into your home.

How to Install a Patio Door

Build a temporary support wall. Use doubled 2 x 4s (or 4 x 4s) for the top plate and support posts. The wall should extend at least 2 ft. past the planned door opening in each direction and cannot be more than 24" away from the bearing wall. Secure the support wall to the floor and to the ceiling.

Remove the old door and the wallcoverings in the project area. If there are light switches or receptacles in the demolition area, shut off their power supply at the main service panel and then remove cover plates. To remove the old door, take off the case molding and then cut through the nails by sawing between the jambs and the frame with a reciprocating saw and bi-metal blade (inset).

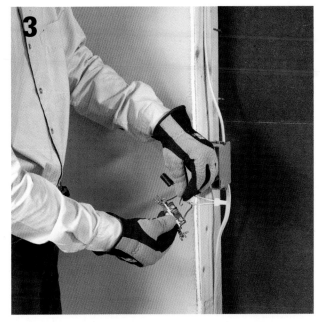

Relocate wiring elements such as switches and receptacles so they are safely outside the new door area. You will need an electrical permit for this and possibly an on-site inspection. If you are not experienced with home wiring, hire an electrician for this part of the job.

Remove wall studs in the project area. If they are difficult to remove, cut them through the center with a reciprocating saw first. Watch out for nails driven in through the exterior side.

(continued)

5

Frame the rough opening so it is sized according to the door manufacturer's recommendation. Install the new king studs if needed and then install the jack studs.

6

King stud

Jack studs

Install the new header by driving 16d nails through the king stud and into the ends of the header. You can make your own structural header by sandwiching a strip of ½" plywood between two pieces of dimensional lumber (inset). Assemble the header with construction adhesive and 10d nails or 2½" deck screws. You can also purchase an engineered header.

7

Cut through the exterior wall materials. You can either mark the corners of the framed opening by driving a nail out from the side, or simply use the framed opening as guidance for your reciprocating saw. Also cut through the sole plate at the edges of the opening so the cut end is flush with the jack stud face.

8

Lift the door unit or frame into the opening, with a helper. Test the fit. Trace the edges of the preattached brickmold onto the outside wall, or place a piece of brickmold next to the door and trace around the perimeter to establish cutting lines (inset). Remove the door.

9

Cut along the brickmold cutting lines with a saw set to a cutting depth equal to the thickness of the siding and the wall sheathing. Finish the cuts at the corners with a handsaw. Thoroughly vacuum the floor in the door opening.

10

Seal the framed opening by installing strips of building paper or self-adhesive rubber flashing product. Make sure that the top strip overlaps any seams you create. If the patio door is exposed, attach drip edge molding to the top of the framed opening.

11

Apply a bead of exterior-rated panel adhesive to the door threshold. Also apply adhesive to the back surface of the preattached brickmold or the nailing flange (whichever your door has).

12

Set the door in position so the brickmold or nailing flange is flush against the outside of the framed opening. Center it in the opening, side to side. Tack the door near the top of each side and then check with a level. Install shims where necessary so the door is plumb. Re-hang the door in the frame, if it has been removed.

13

Fill the gaps around the door with minimal expanding foam or with loosely backed fiberglass insulation (foam makes a better seal). Patch the wall and attach case molding (see pages 194 to 195). If your door does not have preattached brickmold, cut and attach molding on the outside.

Installing Molding

The term *trim* refers to all of the moldings that dress up walls and ceilings, hide gaps and joints between surfaces, and adorn window and door frames. As a decorating tool, trim lends a sculptural quality to otherwise flat surfaces and can have a dramatic effect on any room in the house. Working with trim involves a few specific cuts and techniques, but once you learn them, you can install almost any type.

Crown molding decorates the intersection of walls and ceilings. Most crown molding is sprung, meaning it is installed at an angle to its nailing surfaces, leaving a hollow space behind it. It can be builtup with several styles to create custom looks. In addition to wood, crown molding can be made with plastic polymers, often in ornate, one-piece styles.

Casing is trim that covers the edges of door and window jambs.

Picture rail is a traditional molding that installs parallel to crown molding and has a protruding rounded edge that holds hooks for hanging pictures. Similarly, a chair rail runs horizontally along walls, though at a height of 30 to 36 inches to serve as a border for wallpaper or wainscot, or as a transition between different paint colors. Both chair and picture rail are installed like baseboard.

Baseboard covers the bottoms of walls along the floor. Styles range from single-piece to built-up versions that include a base cap and a base shoe installed at the floor. Base shoe is small, typically rounded molding that is flexible and can follow contours in the floor to hide gaps left by the baseboard.

To avoid problems due to shrinkage after installation, stack the trim in the room where it will be installed and allow it to acclimate for several days. Apply a coat of primer or sealer to all sides of each piece, and let it dry thoroughly before installing it. You may also choose to paint or stain the trim before installing it.

Attach wood trim with finish nails, which have small heads that you drive below the surface using a nail set. Nails for most trim are size 6d or smaller, depending on the thickness of the trim and the wall surface. At a minimum, nails should be long enough to penetrate the framing by at least ¾"; heavier trim requires nails with more holding power. Use finish screws for securing trim to steel studs. After the trim is installed and all the nails are set, fill the nail holes with wood putty, and touch up the areas with paint or stain.

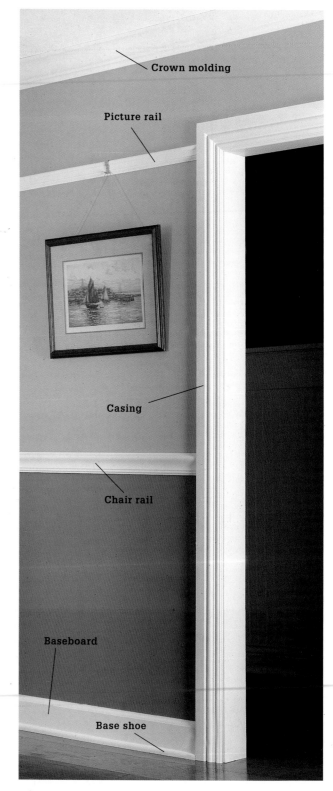

Trim moldings such as case molding and baseboard give a room a sense of completion.

How to Install Baseboard

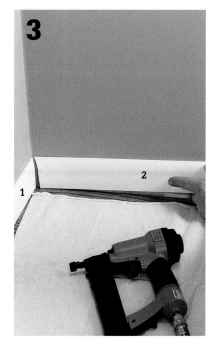

Measure, cut, and install the first piece of baseboard. Butt both ends into the corners tightly. For longer lengths, it is a good idea to cut the piece slightly oversized (up to 1/16" on strips over 10 ft. long) and spring it into place. Nail the molding in place with two nails at every stud location.

Cut the second piece of molding oversized by 6 to 10" and cope cut the adjoining end to the first piece. Fine-tune the cope with a metal file and sandpaper. Dry fit the joint, adjusting it as necessary to produce a tight-fitting joint.

Make the inside corner joint. Use a T-bevel to transfer the proper angle. Cut the second piece (coped) to length and install it with two nails at each stud location.

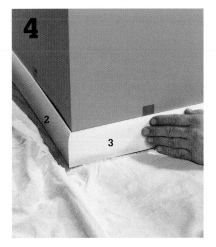

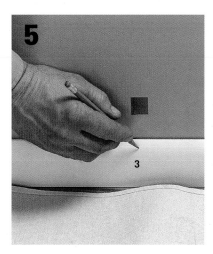

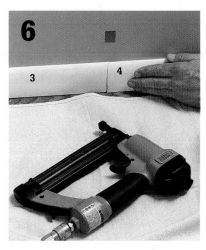

Make the outside corner joint. Test-fit the cut to ensure a tight joint (inset). Remove the mating piece of trim and fasten the first piece for the outside corner joint.

Lay out any scarf joints by placing the piece in position so that the previous joint is tight and then marking the center of a stud location nearest the opposite end. Set the angle of your saw to 30° and cut the molding at the marked location.

Nail the third piece in place, making sure the outside corner joint is tight. Cut the end of the fourth piece to match the scarf joint angle and nail it in place with two nails at each stud location. Add the remaining pieces of molding, fill the nail holes with putty, and apply a final coat of finish.

How to Install Door & Window Case Molding

On each jamb, mark a reveal line ⅛" from the inside edge. The casing will be installed flush with these lines. *Note: You can set the reveal at whatever dimension you choose, but make sure it's equal on all jambs.*

Place a length of casing along one side jamb, flush with the reveal line. At the top and bottom of the molding, mark the points where horizontal and vertical reveal lines meet. (When working with doors, mark the molding at the top only.)

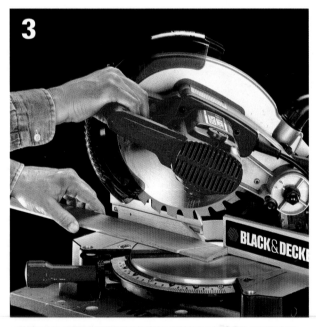

Make 45° miter cuts on the ends of the moldings. Measure and cut the other vertical molding pieces using the same method.

Drill pilot holes spaced every 12" to prevent splitting, and attach the vertical casings with 4d finish nails driven through the casings and into the jambs. For doors, cut the side casings so the bottoms butt against the finished floor (bottom) or a plinth block.

5

Measure the distance between the side casings, and cut top and bottom casings to fit with ends mitered at 45°. If the window or door unit is not perfectly square, make test cuts on scrap pieces to find the correct angle of the joints. Drill pilot holes and attach with finish nails.

Tip ▶

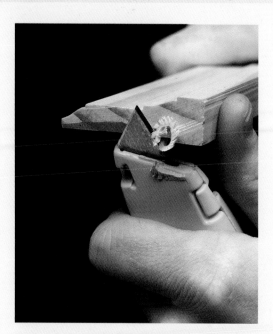

Back-cut the ends of casing pieces where needed using a sharp utility knife to help create tight joints.

6

Locknail the corner joints. Drill pilot holes and drive 4d finish nails through each corner, or drive finishing nails through each corner with a power nailer, as shown. If necessary, drive all nail heads below the wood surface using a nail set, then fill the nail holes with wood putty.

7

Fill nail holes and paint or stain the casings to match the rest of the trim in the room.

BASEMENT
ROOMS

Basement Room Projects

In this chapter you will see eight different basement rooms being constructed. The goal of this chapter is to provide you with a general overview of what each type of room requires and what sorts of problems you can expect to encounter if you choose to add a similar room in your basement. The steps in each project are cross-referenced back to relevant material that has already appeared in this book so you know where to look for more details.

The rooms that are included in this exercise are among the most common basement room projects. A three-quarter bathroom project gives you new detailed information on how to run plumbing lines along with sequencing information on how to organize your bathroom building project. A guest bedroom includes a new egress window and an aromatic cedar-lined closet. A family room project has a detailed feature on installing a vent-free gas fireplace and building a custom surround. The basement laundry center is primarily a demonstration of using stock cabinets to convert a utility space into a clean, efficient area for laundry.

Next, you'll find the basic information for a basement wine cellar, a home gym, and a built-in custom cherry bar.

In this chapter:

- Bathroom
- Guest Bedroom
- Family Room
- Laundry Center
- Wine Cellar
- Gym
- Home Office
- Built-in Bar

A half bath or three-quarter bath (as seen here) is a much-appreciated addition to your basement if you are adding new living spaces elsewhere on the basement level.

Bathroom

Adding a bathroom to an unfinished basement creates a host of new opportunities for finishing the rest of the space. With a convenient bathroom, you can much more easily justify a downstairs recreation room, a wine cellar, a home theater, or additional bedrooms. Many new homes are pre-plumbed with available stub-outs for plumbing at the time the house is built. More likely, you'll need to break up the concrete floor to install a new drain and supply plumbing. This is exactly as much work as it sounds like, but with a jackhammer and some help, it is manageable.

Because horizontal plastic pipes cannot be encased in concrete, they must be laid in the granular fill beneath the concrete basement floor. Possible locations for the bathroom, therefore, are limited by how close the main sewer line is to the floor surface when it meets the main drain stack. Check local codes for other specific restrictions in your area.

Plan ahead for this project. Once you cut into the main waste vent, there can be no drainage in the house until you have fully installed the new branch lines and sealed the joints. Make sure you have extra pipe and fittings on hand.

Sawing and jackhammering concrete (you'll have to do this to run the new pipeline) produces large quantities of dust. Use plastic sheeting to block off other portions of the basement, and wear approved particulate dust masks. Once you've gotten past the chore of running plumbing lines, equipping a bathroom in the basement involves the same work as adding one anywhere else in the house.

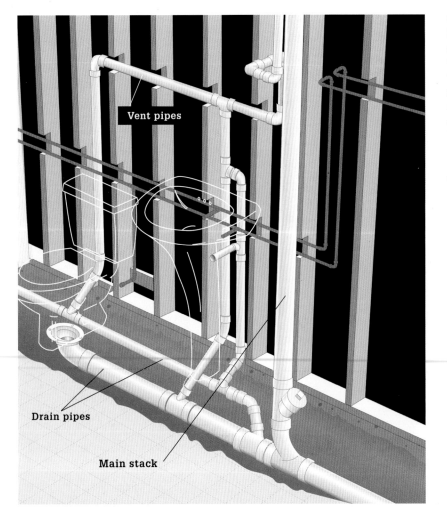

Vent pipes

Drain pipes

Main stack

Our demonstration bathroom includes a shower, toilet, and pedestal sink arranged in a line to simplify trenching. A 2" drainpipe services the new shower and sink; a 3" pipe services the new toilet. The drainpipes converge at a Y-fitting joined to the existing main drain. The toilet and sink have individual vent pipes that meet inside the wet wall before extending up into the attic, where they join the main waste-vent stack.

How to Plumb a Basement Bath

Wet wall location

Mark the proposed location of the basement bathroom on the basement floor using tape. Include the walls, wet wall, and fixture locations. The easiest configuration is to install all the fixtures against the wet wall, which will contain the water supply and vents. The drain lines should run parallel to the wet wall in the most direct route to the main waste-vent stack. Mark the drain line location (typically around 6" out from the wet wall).

Waste-vent stack

Cut out the area around the main stack. Use a concrete saw or a circular saw with a masonry blade to score a 24 × 24" square cutting line around the waste-vent stack. The cut should be at least 1" deep.

Remove concrete and dirt around the main stack. Using a cold chisel and hand maul, strike along the scored cutting lines to chip out the concrete around the main soil stack. If necessary, break up the concrete within the square so it can be removed. Take care not to damage the pipe. Excavate within the square to determine the depth of the sewer line where it meets the main stack.

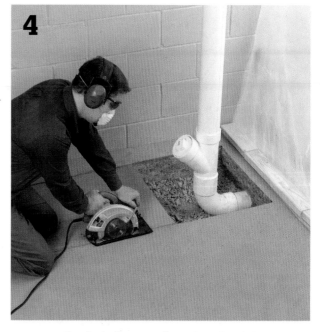

Excavate the drain line trench. Enclose the work area with plastic sheeting to protect the rest of the house from concrete dust. Use a chalk line to lay out a 24"-wide trench centered over the new branch drain location. Score along the lines with a concrete saw or a circular saw with a masonry blade.

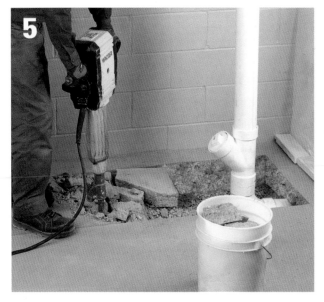

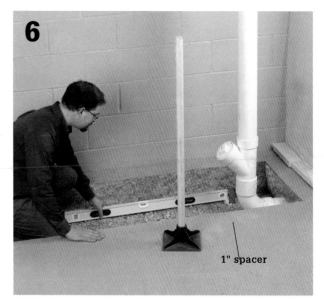

Use a jackhammer to break up the concrete in the trench, taking care not to damage any of the existing plumbing lines. Wear gloves, eye and ear protection, and a dust mask. Remove the concrete for disposal. Remove dirt (technically called granular fill) from the trench, starting at the main waste-vent stack.

Create a flat-bottomed trench that slopes toward the main stack at ¼" per ft. The soil will hold up the drain lines, so it is important to create an even surface. Use a hand tamper to tamp down the soil if it has been disturbed. Tape a 1" spacer to the end of a 4-ft. level to create a handy measuring tool for checking the proper slope. Set the soil aside to use for backfill.

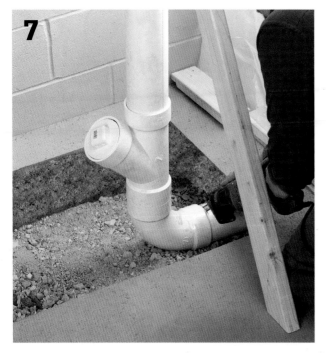

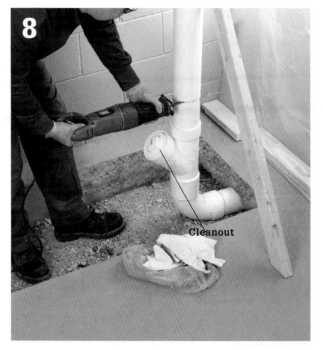

Cut the drain line or main stack (depending on how deep the drain line is) using a reciprocating saw (or a snap cutter). Support the main waste-vent stack before cutting. Use a 2 x 4 and duct tape for a plastic stack, or riser clamps for a cast-iron stack. If cutting the horizontal drain line, cut as close as possible to the stack.

Cut into the stack above the cleanout, and remove the pipe and fittings. Wear rubber gloves, and have a large plastic bag and rags ready, as old pipes and fittings may be coated with sewer sludge. Remember that no wastewater can flow in the house while the pipes are cut open. Turn off the water and drain toilets to prevent accidental use.

(continued)

9

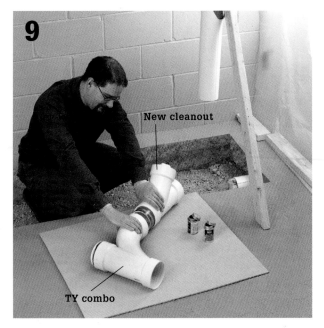

New cleanout

TY combo

Cut and test fit a new cleanout and long sweep TY combo assembly, dry-fitting it to the drain stack and the horizontal drain line to the street. Make any needed adjustments and then solvent-glue the fittings and new pipe into a single assembly.

10

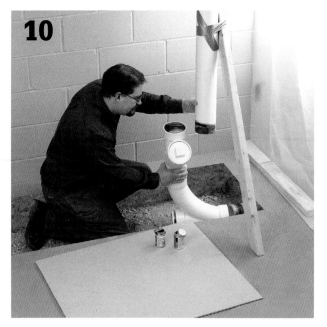

Clean the outside of the old pipes thoroughly and apply primer. Also apply primer and solvent glue to the female surfaces of the union fittings in the assembly. Slide the fitting assembly over the primed ends of the drain stack and the drain line at the same time. This requires a little bit of play in one or both of the lines so you can manipulate the new assembly. If your existing pipes will not move at all, you'll need to use a banded coupling on the drain stack to seal the gap.

11

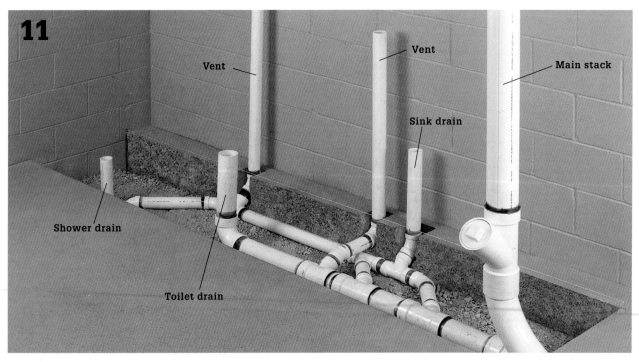

Vent

Vent

Main stack

Sink drain

Shower drain

Toilet drain

Cut and fit the components of the new drain line one piece at a time, starting at the stack. Use strings or boards to outline the wet wall, so vent placement is correct. Drain lines underground must be a minimum of 2". Use 3 × 2" reducing Ys to tie the shower drain line and the sink drain line into the toilet drain line. Install vertical drain and vent lines that are long enough to protrude well above the level of the finished floor.

Check for leaks by pouring water into each new drainpipe. If the joints appear sound, contact your building department and arrange for your inspection (you must do this prior to covering the pipes). Plug the pipe openings with rags to prevent sewer gas from escaping. *Note: Some municipalities require an air test as well.*

Backfill around the pipes with the soil dug from the trench. Mix and pour new concrete to cover the trench, and trowel smooth. Allow the concrete to cure for three days. Some municipalities may require that isolation membrane be wrapped around vertical pipes where they will be surrounded by concrete—check with your local inspector.

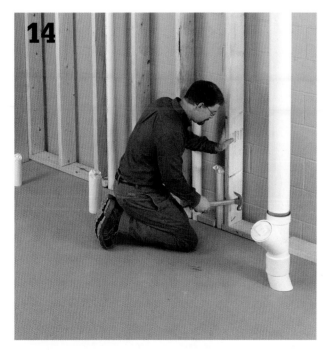

Build the wet wall from 2 × 6 lumber. The sill plate should be pressure treated, but the other members may be SPF. Notch the sill plate so the vent pipes clear it easily. Use masonry anchors or concrete nails and a powder-actuated nailer to attach the plate.

Run 2" vent pipes through notches in the studs. Assemble with vent T and 90° fittings. The 2" pipes are larger than required, but using the same size as the drain lines eliminates the need for reducing fittings and makes for less waste. The 90° fittings are typically less expensive than the vent elbows.

(continued)

16

Route the vent pipe to a point beneath a wall cavity running from the basement to the attic. Or, if there is another vent line closer that you can tie into (not very likely), go ahead and do that.

17

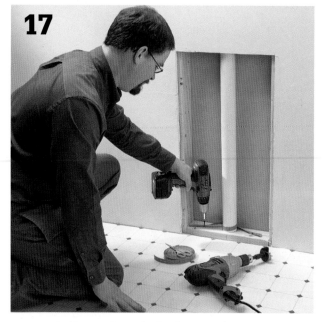

Run vent pipe up through the floors above and either directly out through the roof or tie it to another vent pipe in the attic. Remove sections of wall surface as needed to bore holes for running the vent pipe through wall plates. Feed the vent pipe up into the wall cavity from the basement. Wedge the vent pipe in place while you solvent-glue the fittings. Support the vent pipe at each floor with plastic pipe hangers installed horizontally. Stuff fiberglass insulation into holes around pipes. Do not replace any wall coverings until you have had your final inspection.

18

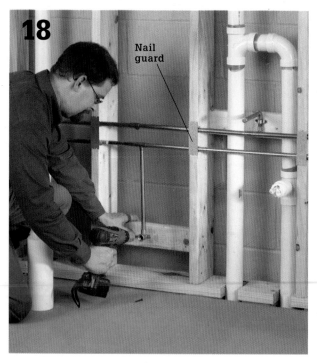

Nail guard

Install the water supply plumbing. Compared to the drain-vent plumbing, this will seem remarkably easy.

Soldering ▶

Use caution when soldering copper. Pipes and fittings become very hot and must be allowed to cool before handling.

How to Build a Basement Bathroom

Frame the new walls using pressure treated sole plates. If walls will contain additional plumbing, build them from 2 x 6 stock.

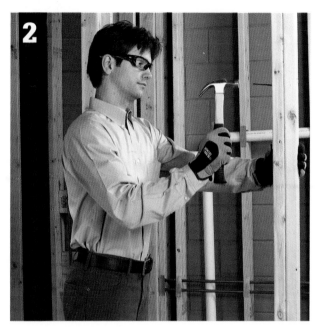

Install framing for the bathroom door (see pages 134 to 135). For economy, a 30"-wide prehung interior door makes sense, but if you want to conserve space consider installing a pocket door (pages 184 to 186). They are fairly common for bathroom applications.

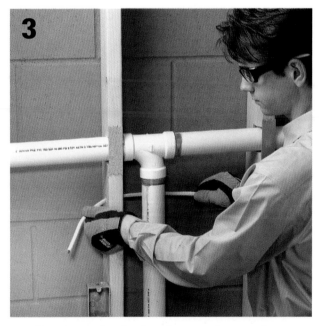

Install 12/2 NM sheathed cable to supply power for a dedicated 20-amp small appliance circuit. Most codes have specific requirements for spacing. The circuit must have GFCI protection. You can wire it with individually protected GFCI receptacles or install a 20-amp GFCI breaker in the main service panel. If you do not have experience with home wiring, hire a professional.

Wire ceiling lights and any wall lights for a lighted medicine chest. Recessed canister lights are a good choice for basements because they don't project down into the room. Have all wiring inspected and approved before you close up the walls.

(continued)

5

Add ventilation. Basement vents require powered vent fans that can be wall-mounted or ceiling mounted (see pages 52 to 55). The ductwork for the fan exhaust is normally routed out through a hole in the rim joist of the house. If the bathroom contains a shower or bathtub, the duct must terminate outdoors. If it is only a half bath some codes allow you to vent into an attic.

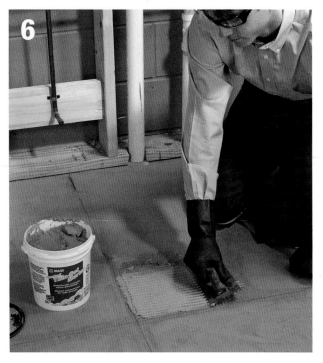

6

Install floor coverings (pages 92 to 122). Here, a bed of thinset mortar is being laid for textured porcelain floor tiles. The mortar bed usually can be applied directly to the concrete floor.

7

Trim floor covering materials to fit around drainpipes in the floor, such as the toilet drain stub-out seen here. Complete the floor covering installation.

8

Install the shower pan according to the manufacturer's instructions. Some are set into a bed of mortar or mastic while others are fastened to the wall framing. Trim the drainpipe to the recommended height first (bottom photo) and make all drain connections.

Install shower supply pipes and make hookups to the faucet body. *Note: The easiest shower stalls to install are freestanding, but kits and tileboard units that are installed in framed alcoves are cheaper. Read the directions that come with your stall to see if they recommend installing panels, such as cementboard, as backer before you install the shower.*

Install the shower enclosure kit or make your custom shower surround with tileboard.

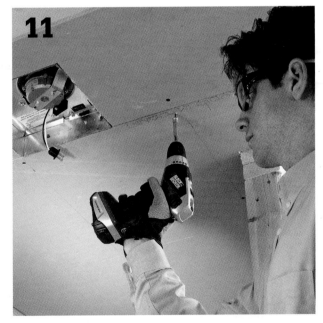

Install ceiling coverings (see pages 160 to 166). While there are advantages to installing a suspended ceiling or acoustic tile ceiling that's easy to remove for access, mold-resistant wallboard is economical, paintable, and has a finished room feel that the other types lack.

Install wall coverings (see pages 142 to 159). Do not use standard wallboard. Use mold-resistant wallboard or cementboard throughout. Do not install a vapor barrier behind the wallboard.

(continued)

Attach any other wall-mounted fixtures, such as the pedestal sink being hung on a mounting plate above. Do all of the work requiring access to wall or ceiling stud cavities before you install the wall coverings. And don't neglect to have inspections done.

Cover seams and fill holes in the walls and ceiling with fiberglass wallboard tape and joint compound (see pages 152 to 155). Sand the compound smooth and apply a coat of wallboard primer.

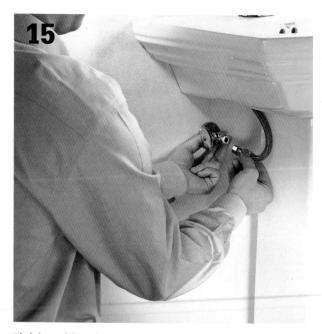

Finish making the supply and drain hookups for the lavatory. Add faucets to all fixtures and test them.

Install the toilet after trimming the closet drain pipe to the correct height. Hook up the water supply to the fill valve and then test the operation. Drain times can be a bit slower in basements, and flushes may be weakened slightly by the shallowness of the drain line slopes.

17

Paint the walls and ceiling using a paint with a mold-resistant additive. Paint the ceiling first. For bathrooms, choose a washable, semigloss paint.

18

Hang the entry door and install trim around the door as well as a baseboard trim (see pages 192 to 195). You may find it easier to paint or finish the door and trim before installation.

19

Install mirrors, medicine cabinets, towel rods, paper holders, and any other members of the decorative bathroom suite.

20

Attach trim kits and escutcheons to light fixtures and vent fans. Add switch plates and receptacle covers, too. Test all fixtures.

A large closet lined with aromatic cedar plus an egress window on the adjoining wall make this basement bedroom safe, convenient, and comfortable.

Guest Bedroom

A basement is a great location for a kid's bedroom or a guest bedroom. In the case of the former, both you and your children will appreciate the space and the small amount of separation that a basement bedroom provides. A basement also makes a good location for a guest room that offers comforts and hospitality yet affords some privacy for your visitors. If you don't expect your guest room to get a lot of users, consider designing it as a multipurpose room that performs other duties, such as working as a home office or a craft room.

Any room that has a closet or is attached to a bathroom is considered a bedroom, regardless of what you may call it on your permit application. Your building department is especially concerned about bedrooms, and it is easy to understand why. Sleeping rooms are in use when we are in our most vulnerable state, so they must be set up for our

protection. That's why any basement bedroom must have an egress window that meets minimum size and accessibility requirements (see pages 168 to 172). A smoke detector is also required, and a radon detector is highly recommended (radon levels are highest in the basement). Bedrooms also must be comfortable. In basements that means providing ample heat, perhaps a dehumidifier and a warm floor. Carpeting isn't always a great choice for basements, but it is a very nice feature for bedrooms and there are certain types that work fine (see pages 110 to 121).

A closet is a very important part of any bedroom. As you'll see in the following pages, it is easy to build and equip. *Note: If you are installing a closet light be sure to make it one that uses bulbs that do not produce a lot of heat. Fluorescent bulbs are required for closets in many areas.*

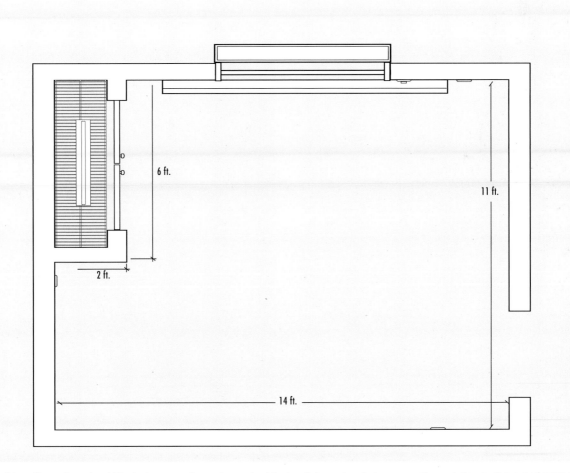

A working floorplan should include room dimensions, electrical outlets and switches, as well as windows, doors and permanent features such as closets.

How to Build a Guest Bedroom

1

Replace small basement windows with at least one egress window that is large enough to allow an adult to exit (see pages 174 to 175). Codes are absolutely clear that any inhabited room must have egress. Enlarge the window opening.

2

Install a new window that meets code requirements for egress (see page 21) and install a code-compliant window well on the exterior side.

3

Build all four stud walls, fastening sole plates to the concrete floor with a powder-actuated tool (see pages 126 to 127). Walls built next to exterior walls should be stopped ½" short of the wall to prevent direct contact. Do not install vapor barriers (see pages 42 to 47).

4

Build the partition walls to frame the closet. Closets should be at least 32" deep from front to back. Walk-in closets are deeper. This closet will be equipped with a louvered bifold door, but it would also be a good place to install a pocket door (see pages 184 to 187).

Install light fixture boxes in the room's ceiling and closet. Consider what type of ceiling you'll be installing when positioning the fixtures. Recessed canister lights work well in a room. In closets, however, most codes require that only fluorescent or compact fluorescent bulbs are used because of the potential of incandescent bulbs to overheat in confined spaces.

Install the room wiring according to codes for minimum receptacle spacing and switch locations (see pages 56 to 57). Basement bedrooms do not require GFCI-protected receptacles, but they are a good idea nonetheless.

Add heating and cooling as needed (see pages 48 to 51). An electric baseboard heater is a frequent choice for basement rooms. Look for a model with a wall-mounted thermostat. While 120-volt heaters are available, 240-volt models are much more energy efficient. You will need to provide 240-volt service of course, usually in a 20-amp or 30-amp circuit, depending on the number of feet of heater you install.

Install mold-resistant wallboard on all walls, making sure the bottoms of the panels are at least ½" above the floor (see page 148). Do not insulate exterior walls. You may insulate interior walls for soundproofing, however. Use unfaced fiberglass batts or rigid foam boards (fiberglass is a better soundproofer but rigid foam is less hospitable to mold). *Note: Have preliminary wiring inspections done before closing up walls.*

(continued)

9

Line the closet walls. Here, aromatic cedar paneling is being installed on the closet interior, and standard mold-resistant wallboard is going onto the room side of the walls. Cedar is naturally resistant to moisture-related rot.

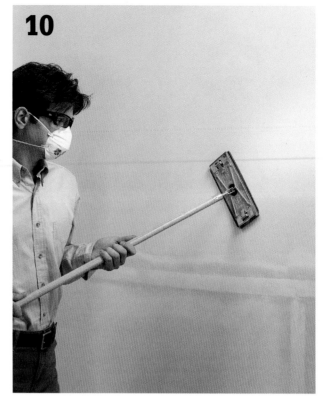

10

Finish the walls by taping seams and covering tape and screwheads with joint compound (see pages 150 to 157). Apply a coat of primer and then paint.

11

Install the remaining electrical fixtures and make wiring hookups (see pages 62 to 65). The electric baseboard heater being installed here (see pages 50 to 51) is sited beneath the window because that is the most efficient location for a heater. Have final electrical inspections performed.

12

Install a ceiling. Here, acoustic tile is being installed over wood furring strips that have been attached to the ceiling (see pages 164 to 165). Acoustic tile helps soundproof the bedroom from foot traffic on the first floor. Look for mold-resistant tiles, preferably with vinyl surface coatings.

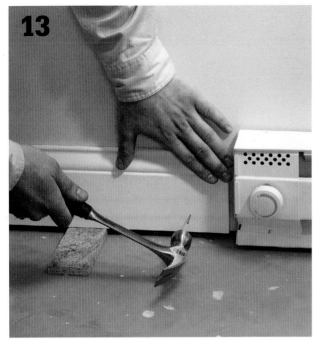

13

Install trim, including baseboard trim and window and door trim (see pages 192 to 195). Maintain a gap of at least ½" between base trim and baseboard heaters. Prepaint or stain the trim pieces before installation for a neater job. Egress windows can be trimmed with custom jambs and casing (see pages 176 to 179).

14

Install closet shelves. Closet organizers made from vinyl-coated wire are good choices for basements because they allow maximum air circulation and will not contribute to mold or mildew problems.

15

Install the closet door (see page 187). A bifold door with louvers is a good choice for basement bedroom closets because it allows ventilation. Louvers can be time-consuming to paint, however. To simplify the painting, paint the door in a well-ventilated room using an HVLP paint sprayer before installing it.

16

Install floor coverings (see pages 92 to 121). Carpet isn't always a great choice for basements, but if you have not had significant water problems consider it for a bedroom, where a soft, warm floor is a big benefit. Use a moisture-resistant, solid rubber pad. Carpeting with synthetic fibers is recommended.

This cozy family room features a vent-free gas fireplace and a brand new patio door that opens out to a lower level walkout patio.

Family Room

The family room is the only type of room that is actually getting larger as a percentage of the total floorspace in today's new homes. Whether we use it for watching movies, playing games, or just hanging out reading, the family room is an important place in any home. A well-designed family room is spacious, has good light, features comfortable floors, and is easy to clean. It can include a few luxurious features such as a fireplace, a mini-kitchen with snack area, a home theater setup, or a dry bar.

One important consideration when designing a family room is traffic flow. This is especially important if your family room will have exterior access like the walk-out patio door seen here. Try to arrange the room so that a line drawn from the main entry point from upstairs to the exterior door doesn't split the room in two. Be a bit protective of the floorplan so you can set up furniture or arrange activities that can proceed without constant interruptions as other family members move from door to door.

As you design your room, also take into account the electronics that will be set up in your room. Installing high-speed computer/television cable lines, speaker wire, phone lines, and other forms of structured wiring is easiest to do when the walls are uncovered.

The family room seen here features a vent-free gas fireplace. It is not a significant heat source. If you are interested in a fireplace that can provide supplemental heat, install a direct-vent gas fireplace or a woodburning one instead.

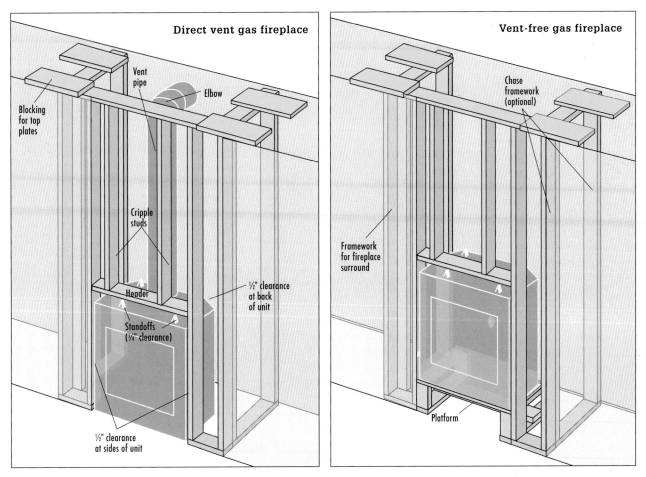

Gas fireplaces come in two types for home use: direct vent (left), which must be exhausted to the home exterior, and vent-free, which do not require venting but must be installed in either an existing firebox or a specially designed firebox that circulates air and exhaust internally. Vent-free models are not currently allowed in the Upper Midwest, California, Alaska, Hawaii, or Canada.

How to Build a Family Room with Fireplace

1

Frame the new walls for the room (see pages 128 to 139). Here, an open area in a walkout basement with a finished exterior wall is being divided into a smaller finished space for a family room with direct access to a patio.

2

Install wiring cables in the stud walls (see pages 162 to 165). Because family rooms normally include several types of electronic devices, consider adding multimedia outlets for coaxial cable, speaker cables, and phone/high-speed DSL lines. These can be run individually or networked through a distribution center.

3

Install fixture boxes for lights keeping the planned ceiling material thickness and installation method in mind (see pages 62 to 65). Here, a box is being installed for a 6-ft. section of halogen track lighting to provide adjustable lighting that can be focused on the fireplace mantel.

4

Frame the opening for the firebox according to the manufacturer's directions and minimum clearances. Because the fireplace surround planned for this room uses 12 x 12" wall tile around the opening, we added full-height studs so the required cementboard backer can be seamed with the wallboard over a stud. A header for the opening is supported by short jack studs at the sides.

5

Construct a support platform for the firebox. Because the firebox will be housed in open space on the other side of the fireplace wall, we were able to get by with a simple wood platform built with 2 x 4s and ¾" plywood.

Secure the firebox platform in the wall opening by nailing or screwing it to the studs at the edges of the opening. Some manufacturers may require that you secure the platform to the floor as well.

7

Install wallboard on ceiling (see page 147). When wallboarding both the ceiling and the walls, it is usually recommended that you do the ceiling first so the vertical panels can be butted up against the ceiling to provide some extra support. If you are hanging a suspended or tile ceiling, wallboard the walls first.

8

Cut cementboard into strips equal in width to the dimension of your tiled surround and attach them to the 2 x 4 nailers bordering the framed firebox opening. It is generally a good idea to predrill for cementboard screws, especially with narrower strips.

(continued)

9

Install mold-resistant wallboard in the rest of the room, keeping the bottom edges at least ½" above the floor (see page 148). If you have planned your firebox framing properly, all wallboard edges will fall over studs or cross blocks.

10

Apply joint compound and fiberglass seam tape over seams and cover screwheads with compound (see pages 152 to 157). Sand the compound smooth.

11

Prime and paint the ceiling and the walls. To boost the visual interest of the ceiling, we added some texture to the ceiling paint (above) and applied it with a ⅝" nap roller. The effect is much subtler than the iconic cottage cheese ceiling of the 1960s and 70s.

12

Apply a mortar bed for the tile surround using a notched trowel (a ¼" square-notch trowel is typical but check the recommendations on the thinset package label). Apply only as much mortar as you can tile in about 10 minutes. Treating each leg of the square surround separately is a good strategy.

13

Press the surround tiles into the mortar bed and set them by pressing with a short piece of 2 x 4 wrapped in a soft cloth. Most tiles (12 x 12 glass tiles in a mosaic pattern are shown here) have spacing nubs cast into the edges so setting the gaps between tiles or tile sheets is automatic. If your tiles do not have spacing nubs, use plastic tile spacers available at your tile store. Let the thinset mortar dry overnight once you're finished setting the tiles. See page 92 if you need to cut tiles.

14

Apply dark-tinted grout to the tiles using a grout float. Let the grout harden slightly and then buff off the residue with a soft, clean cloth. For more information on grouting, see page 95.

15

Begin adding surround trim. Here, 1 x 4 cherry casing is being attached to wall stud locations. The side casings should be slightly off the floor (if you have not installed flooring yet account for the floor covering thickness) and butted against the tile surround. If you have planned properly, there will be wall studs behind the casing. *Note: We chose 1 x 4 cherry because it is attractive, but also because you can usually buy it dimensioned, planed, and sanded on all sides at the lumber yard. If you have woodworking equipment, use any lumber you like.*

16

Add built-up head casing. The head casing should overhang the side casings by an inch or so. We used a built-up technique to add some depth and profile to the head casing. First, attach a full-width 1 x 4 to the wall. Then, install a 1 x 3 so the ends and top are flush with the ends and top of the 1 x 4. Finally, install a cherry 1 x 2 in the same manner.

(continued)

17

Cut and install the mantel board. We used another piece of 1 x 4 cherry the same length as the head casings, but if you have access to woodworking tools consider a thicker board for a little more presence. Or, face-glue two 1 x 4s together.

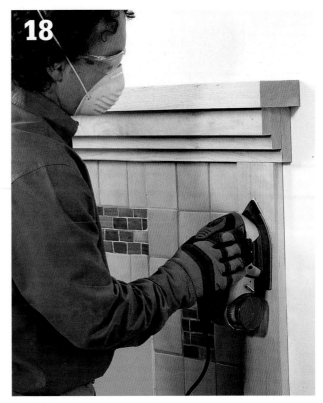

18

Finish-sand all the cherry and then apply a light wood stain. After the stain dries, topcoat with a cherry-tone or light mahogany wipe-on varnish that will even out the uneven coloration typical with cherry. Fill nail holes with cherry-tinted wood putty.

19

Set the firebox for the fireplace into the finished surround and check for level. Fasten it to the framing by nailing or screwing through the nailing flange, depending on the manufacturer's recommendations.

20

Seal the gap around the firebox with high-temperature silicone sealant. Do not use ordinary caulk here because it could melt or even catch fire.

21

Run natural gas supply pipe to within 18" or so of the gas inlet port on the side of the firebox. Attach a stop cock to the supply tube. *Warning: Working with gas pipe and making gas hookups is very dangerous and in many municipalities it may only be done by a licensed professional. Doing the work yourself may also void the warranty on your gas appliance. It is strongly recommended that you hire a professional for this part of the project.*

22

Connect the fireplace to the gas supply with a flexible gas connector tube, making sure to use gas-rated teflon tape to lubricate screw threads on the connector. Restore the gas supply and test all connections with leak detector spray (inset).

23

Install floor coverings. Snap-together laminate planks are easy to install and in general a good choice for basement family rooms (see pages 96 to 99). Trim the laminate planks to fit around the fireplace casings.

24

Install baseboard moldings (see pages 192 to 195), lighting trim kits, and any other finishing trim such as door casings (see pages 192 to 195). Remember to read the vent-free fireplace manual thoroughly and follow all safety precautions for operation. Have the unit inspected annually to make sure it is still operating properly.

Laundry Center

Many of the areas where we do our laundry lack two important features: organization and lighting. This basement laundry center is a self-contained built-in that functions like a room within a room, adding both storage space and task lighting for what can otherwise be a disagreeable task. It is built from a base cabinet and butcher block countertop on one side of a 24"-wide, seven-foot-tall stub wall, and a bank of wall cabinets on the other side of the wall. The cabinets are designed to fit above a washer and dryer combo. The structure includes a ceiling with light fixtures mounted over both sides, and a switch wired into the stub wall to control the lights. The walls are built from inexpensive wall sheathing and, along with the ceiling, are clad with easy-to-wash tileboard

that adds brightness while contrasting with the maple wood of the cabinets. The edges of the center are trimmed with clear maple.

If you are creating your built-in laundry center in a room that did not previously house your washer and dryer, arrange for and have installed the hookups for both appliances before you build. If you are not experienced with plumbing and wiring, hire a plumber and electrician to run any new drain, supply, dryer vent, or electrical service lines. Also make sure to identify potential sources for electrical service to power the lights (in the version seen here, we installed recessed canister lights over the countertop and above the washer and dryer).

Some stock cabinets and some carpentry skills are the main tools you need to convert a basement room into an efficient laundry center.

Install a Recessed Washing Machine Box ▸

A recessed washing machine box not only makes your laundry area neater, it reduces the chances of damaging supply connections. If the box includes an opening for the washing machine drain hose, it must be located near a utility sink so you can tie into the sink drain with a standpipe (see right). Normally the hot and cold hose bibs (faucets) in the washing machine box tie into nearby supply tubes for the utility sink. But you can splice into any supply lines that are convenient.

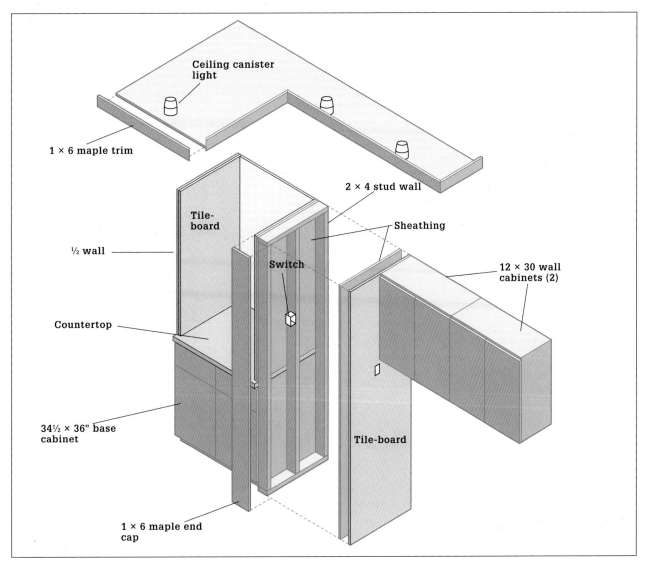

The framework for this laundry center is a 2-ft-wide by 7-ft.-tall stub wall. The ironing area is a standard base cabinet with a butcher block countertop, and the center is covered with an L-shaped panel containing task lighting. A bank of wall cabinets fits over the machine locations.

How to Build a Laundry Center

Frame and finish laundry room walls and then attach the sole plate for the partition wall. Locate the wall so the base cabinet (here, 36" wide) will fit between the clad stub wall and the room wall.

Attach the cap plate and studs to finish the stub wall framing. The wall stud that fits against the back wall should fall over a stud location for sturdy fastening. If it does not, you'll need to cut open the wall and install 2 x 4 blocking between studs to tie into.

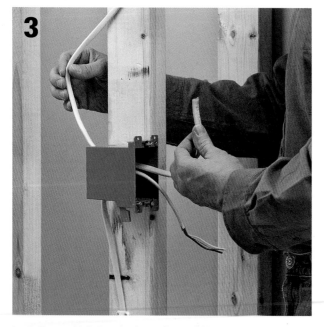

Install a switch box in the wall at 48" high to house the switch for the task lights, if you wish to include them. Run nonmetallic sheathed cable through holes in the studs making sure to staple it within 8" of the box. Run cable to the power source but don't hook it up yet. Run cable from the switch to the junction box or boxes in the task lighting fixtures.

Install a base cabinet (36" wide as shown) between the stub wall and the corner of the room. Anchor the cabinet by driving screws into framing members on each side. For the most pleasing results, choose a base cabinet that matches the wall cabinets you'll be installing over the laundry machines.

5

Cut a piece of countertop to fit and attach it to the top nailing strips on the base cabinet. Choose a material with a nice smooth surface that is easy to clean. Butcher block is shown here, but a less extravagant material like postform will do.

6

Stud location

Attach a strip of ½" plywood sheathing to the corner wall to make a spacer/backer for the tileboard surface. Drive wallboard screws at stud locations. Apply a few beads of panel adhesive to the back of the panel first for extra holding power.

7

Also attach plywood sheathing to the stub wall framing. Make a cutout for the light switch box on the laundry machine side of the stub wall.

8

Cut strips of tileboard to fit the wall surfaces, and attach them with panel adhesive. Rub back and forth over the tileboard surface with a clean rag to set the bond. If any tileboard sticks out past the wall edges, trim it off with a utility knife.

(continued)

9

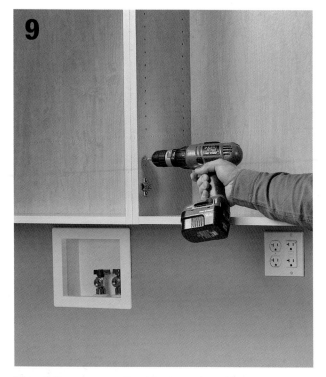

Mount the upper wall cabinets so the cabinet tops are flush with the top of the stub wall. You can tack a temporary ledger to the wall directly below the cabinets to support them while you install fasteners. Drive screws through the nailing strips in the backs of the cabinets at wall stud locations. Then, fasten the cabinet to one another with a few ⅞" screws.

10

Cut a piece of plywood sheathing so it will fit over the laundry folding area and the wall cabinets—this will have an L shape in most cases. Create enough overhang in front of the wall cabinets that you can mount small recessed task light if you choose. Glue tileboard to the underside of the ceiling to make a clean, bright surface.

11

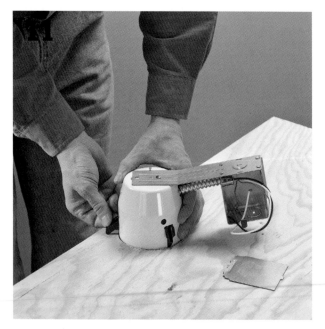

Make cutouts and mount the light fixture to the ceiling panel before you install it. Look for low-profile canister lights to fit the space. Here, one light is positioned over the folding area and two are recessed above the wall cabinets. They are wired together in series.

12

Attach the ceiling panel to the top of the stub wall and to the wall cabinet tops. Also secure it to the top of the backer panel in the corner.

13

Make the wiring hookups at the light fixtures and at the switch. Shut off power at the main service panel and connect the power lead to your power source. Restore power and test the lights.

14

Attach strips of 1 x 4 hardwood (maple is seen here) to conceal top gaps and create a visual baffle for the light cans. You can find premilled hardwood at most lumber yards in standard dimensions.

15

Attach hardwood strips to cover the front of the stub wall. Attach narrower strips to cover the edges of the backer and tileboard in the corner. This strip should run from the countertop to the underside of the ceiling trim strip.

16

Install your washer and dryer. Front-loading models work best in this situation because they create convenient horizontal surfaces. But top loaders will also fit.

Wine Cellar

You can build a wine cellar anywhere in your home, but it makes most sense in a basement where temperature, humidity, and light levels are easier to control. When stored in a dark, cool, well-ventilated area where the temperature and relative humidity are fairly constant, wine improves with age. For the serious vinophile, a successful wine cellar must be a controlled environment. The temperature, humidity, and light levels need to be kept within narrow ranges to safeguard a wine collection. After the environment is established, the issues of storage, such as racking, management, and appreciation of the collection, must be addressed. But if you also hope to use your wine cellar as a living space for tasting and casual dining, all of this controlling of the environment must be balanced with the requirements for creating a comfortable home.

Wine racks are the backbone of any wine cellar. If you are a skilled carpenter or woodworker, making your own wine racks is a fun exercise in designing and building. But if your ambition outpaces your experience, look into purchasing and installing a modular wine rack system. Sold over the Internet and at design centers, these systems allow you to design and install custom wine racks that fit your space, but at a fraction of the cost of hiring a professional carpenter to do the job. Most wine rack websites have planning software so you can create the exact design you want.

Basements are ideal locations for wine cellars. Installing a modular wine rack system is a great way to make your cellar look like a professional installation.

How to Create a Wine Cellar

1

Install walls and door as in any of the previous projects. If you are planning a wine cellar that's climate controlled, insulate the interior walls. Do not insulate walls that abut exterior foundation walls (see pages 46 to 47).

2

Install floor coverings (see pages 92 to 121). Ceramic or porcelain tile, like the travertine tile seen here, is a great choice for wine cellars, especially if it has an old-world appearance.

3

Design your wine rack system and order the components. Typical components you can choose from include full-height racks with a separate cubby for each bottle; box- or diamond-shaped racks; curved racks; quarter-round racks; corner racks; racks with tasting shelves, and more. Open the containers and inspect the parts when the kit arrives. Make sure there is no damage and that nothing is missing.

4

The package will include complete assembly instructions. Base your assembly on these. To build the arrangement shown here, we started with the full-height rack, identifying the ladder-shaped standards and orienting them with the bottom ends aligned. The standards should be set parallel on a flat surface.

(continued)

5

Attach spacer bars to the backs of the ladders at the prescribed rung locations using finish nails or air-driven brad nails.

Wood Selection Tips ▶

Modular wine rack kits typically are sold in three or four wood species: cedar, redwood, red oak, and mahogany. The species you select will have a small effect on pricing, but the decision is primarily an aesthetic one. Western red cedar does not have an aromatic cedar scent but is a clear, open-pored wood that produces a beautiful mellow wood tone and does not require topcoating. Redwood is similar to cedar but a bit denser and lighter in tone and with more limited availability. Red oak is harder and heavier and in most cases is stained and topcoated. Mahogany varies quite a bit, based on the country of origin (Malaysia and the Philippines, for example). It is a classic, open-pore wood with straight grain and good resistance to rot.

6

Lift the ladders and spacer bar assembly so it is upright. Insert intermediate ladders between the end ladders you have connected with the spacer bars, following the manufacturer's recommended spacing. Attach the intermediate ladders to the front spacer bars (as shown), according to the manufacturer's instructions.

7

Continue to build the structure by adding the next ladder, repeating steps 5 and 6.

8

Finish attaching the final front spacer bars, and then move the unit into the desired place against the wall. Attach the assembly to the wall using 2½" screws driven through the back spacer bars. Make sure the assembly is level first, and drive the screws at wall stud locations (or use masonry anchors if walls are made of concrete or block).

9

Assemble the next modular unit according to the installation instructions. Position it next to the first unit, level it, and attach it to the wall. Some systems may suggest that you attach it to the first unit as well or that you install a trim piece to conceal the joint where they are connected. Continue installing modular units in the selected order.

10

Attach the last modular unit according to the installation instructions. Also install any trim pieces to conceal gaps between units and between the end unit and the wall. Most wood modular rack systems are either prefinished or designed to remain unfinished. Begin loading your wine collection into the racks.

Countertop Wine Racks ▸

Supplement your large custom wine racking with a few small countertop racks. This is especially handy if you wish to set aside a flight of wine for a tasting party. Small racks like these are also easy and fun projects to build in your shop.

Creating & Using Your Wine Cellar

Starting with the right structure simplifies the process of establishing and maintaining the necessary temperature and humidity in your wine cellar. Choose a location for your wine cellar that meets or can be modified to meet the following requirements.

Walls and ceiling: Because the environment inside the wine cellar is deliberately manipulated to meet certain specific requirements, you'll want to make sure the room is well insulated. This not only allows you to control temperature and humidity more precisely, it helps you do it more efficiently. The walls should be insulated to a minimum of R-19, and the ceiling should be insulated to a minimum of R-30. All of the walls and the ceiling should have a 6 mil polyethylene vapor barrier on the warm side of the insulation. If the wine cellar is cooler than the surrounding area of the house, a vapor barrier should go between the insulation and the rest of the house; if the wine cellar is bordered by an exterior wall do not use a vapor barrier.

Flooring: Moisture-resistant surfaces, such as stone, tile, or brick, are ideal. Stone and tile floors should have a high-friction coefficient so they don't become treacherous if moisture accumulates on them. Hardwood or cork are also appropriate.

Door: An exterior-grade door with weather stripping and a plate seal keeps the conditioned air inside the wine cellar. Glass doors should, at a minimum, be double paned.

TEMPERATURE

For a collector of wine, the most important aspect of a wine cellar is the temperature, which should be kept as constant as possible and between 50°F and 55°F. Any fluctuations should be very gradual because when exposed to temperature swings, the cork material and the bottle expand and contract, which can damage the cork seal and let oxygen into the bottle.

Wine stored at higher temperatures ages faster than wine stored at lower temperatures. Wine develops complexity as it ages, which means that slower is better. The temperature in your cellar should not drop below 50°F, however, or the wine may develop deposits and other suspensions. If you plan to use the cellar as living space, you will probably need to make some concessions on the relatively cool ideal temperature so the room can be enjoyed comfortably.

In large wine cellars, a cooling unit typically is employed to maintain optimum temperatures. Most bear a resemblance to a room air conditioner, but in addition to cooling they also regulate humidity levels.

Typical wood wine racks are constructed from moisture-resistant wood, such as redwood, western red cedar, or mahogany.

Ventilation ▸

A well-ventilated wine cellar is a pleasant place to spend time, for you and for your wine. Odors develop in poorly ventilated space, and those odors may be absorbed by corks and even infiltrate the bottles. You can improve ventilation and air circulation by installing an exhaust fan.

Poor ventilation can destroy wine over time. Adding an exhaust fan safeguards your collection and makes the cellar a more pleasant place. Exhaust fans are available in stylish light/fan combination products (as shown here).

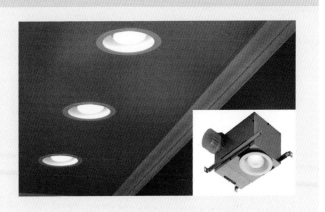

If cooling the entire room isn't practical, consider buying a wine refrigerator. Wine refrigerators are available in sizes designed to hold everything from six to several hundred bottles. Some are quite attractive, too.

RELATIVE HUMIDITY

The relative humidity in a wine cellar should stay between 50 and 80 percent, with the ideal level being 70 percent. At lower humidity levels, corks can shrink and let air into the bottles. Higher levels of humidity won't necessarily harm the wine, but they do encourage the growth of mold and mildew in the room.

Wine should be stored at a temperature of 50°F to 55°F and a humidity level ideally around 70%.

LIGHT

Light, especially sunlight, can damage wine and cause it to develop unpleasant odors. Low levels of light are best, and incandescent or sodium vapor lights are better than fluorescent. Sparkling wines and wines in clear bottles are quite sensitive to light; wines in dark bottles are less susceptible.

Consider controlling the cellar's lights with motion-activated switches. The lights will come on the moment you step into the room and turn off moments after you leave.

If your cellar has windows, block their light as completely as possible. White roller shades block 80 percent of the light and heat gain from windows, so they make good first layers for window coverings. Top the roller shades with blackout draperies or louvered wood shutters, and you've got a winning combination.

VIBRATION

Vibration disturbs the sediment in wine, which can harm it over time. However, unless your home is next to a race track or a rail yard, it's unlikely that vibration will be an ongoing problem. It certainly makes sense to secure your wine racks to the walls or floor to protect them during earthquakes or other disasters, but if the worst happens, it's unlikely that the disruption of sediment will be the biggest problem you face.

Remember, though, that sounds are vibrations, too. The wine cellar should be located as far as possible from, for example, a home theater equipped with surround sound or the practice room for your garage band. If these spaces have to be within close proximity, soundproof them carefully.

Gym

A home gym is more than a few pieces of little-used exercise equipment stashed in a vacant room. To make the leap to being an enjoyable workout room, your gym needs to be in a convenient, accessible space with good lighting, adequate ventilation, and comfortable flooring. It should have adequate electrical supply for a stereo and other entertainment components, as well as powered exercise equipment. It should be a pleasant space that's wisely outfitted to suit your needs.

The basement is a popular location for home gyms. If you plan to build your gym in a basement, check the ceiling height. The ceiling should be at least seven feet, but preferably eight feet high to provide enough headroom for equipment and for stretching.

Unless circumstances—and your budget—allow for superior soundproofing, don't force the gym to share a common wall with an occupied bedroom. Working out can get pretty noisy, what with the clanking of weights, the pounding rhythm of music, or the television cranked up so it can be heard over the whir of the treadmill.

Choose a location large enough to accommodate the equipment you own or plan to include, with plenty of access so you can use it comfortably. Diagram your potential location and possible arrangements of your equipment. Here is a list of some basic equipment and the space required for each.

Equipment Space Requirements ▸

- Treadmill: 30 sq ft.
- Single-station gym: 35 sq ft.
- Free weights: 20 to 50 sq ft.
- Bike: 10 sq ft.
- Rowing machines: 20 sq ft.
- Stair climbers: 10 to 20 sq ft.
- Ski machines: 25 sq ft.
- Multistation gym: 50 to 200 sq ft.

A relatively cool atmosphere and enough elbow room to work out and make a little noise are two of the qualities that make basements good locations for home gyms.

Lighting

A flattering lighting plan is an important part of a home gym. Good lighting makes everyone look better. Looking good takes you several steps toward feeling good, and, as we all know, feeling good makes it easier to take on the challenges of the world, including an exercise plan.

Low-voltage track lights are especially good options for a home gym because they generate pleasant, focusable light without producing as much heat as standard track lighting. It may be appropriate to include some overhead fluorescent lights, but don't limit your lighting plan to those fixtures. Add some incandescent side or uplights, too, to balance shadows and the color of the ambient light.

Installing plenty of mirrors will enhance available light as well as allow you to monitor your form and posture.

Ventilation

If your home gym has operable windows, ventilation shouldn't be a big problem. If it doesn't, mechanical ventilation will make the space more comfortable and pleasant. Installing an exhaust fan on a wall or in the ceiling will help remove moisture and unpleasant odors from the air.

Select a fan sized to provide adequate ventilation for the gym's square footage. According to The Home Ventilating Institute, the air in rooms other than kitchens and bathrooms should be replaced at least six times per hour; the replacement rate recommended for a kitchen is fifteen times an hour and eight times an hour for bathrooms. These are, of course, minimums, and a home gym has unique ventilation needs. You might want to discuss the project with a heating/ventilation/and air conditioning (HVAC) expert before selecting an exhaust fan.

Flooring

Home gym floors have to be comfortable, durable, and easy to clean. Hardwood floors have some of the necessary give and clean up beautifully, but they have a tendency to get scuffed, scratched, and damaged easily. Carpet offers a fairly forgiving and durable surface, but keeping it clean can be a challenge in a gym.

Resilient flooring is one of the best options for floor covering in a home gym. Rubber flooring is particularly appropriate in a home gym: it's easy on the knees, simple to clean, and tough enough to stand up to hard use.

If your floor covering is not ideal and changing it is not an option, place large rubber antifatigue mats (you can buy them at building centers as well as at flooring stores) in critical areas.

Gym flooring should be cushiony enough for comfort yet firm enough that there is only minimal bounce. Rubber floor tiles are a good choice.

Fitness Equipment for Basement Gyms ▸

Most experts agree that life's too short and time too precious to deal with cheap equipment. And, while it's often true that you get what you pay for, the most expensive products are not always the best. Research equipment online, consult retailers, and talk with fitness experts to determine what best meets your needs.

Populating a home gym is largely a matter of choosing equipment that can help you reach your goals. Some types of equipment help you build strength and muscle mass (resistance bands, weight machines, free weights); others help you improve cardiovascular fitness (treadmills, elliptical trainers, stationary bikes). Most of today's professional trainers recommend building core strength as well as doing cardiovascular and weight training.

Diagram the placement of the equipment you plan to include. Next, plan to place electrical outlets as necessary to serve not only the equipment you have but any you hope to add over time. Equipment to consider:

- Swiss (or stability) balls ($20 to $40) help you improve core muscle strength, balance, and stability.
- Resistance bands ($10 to $20) come in different strengths, usually indicated by colors. These bands help you lengthen, strengthen, and tone your muscles.
- Balance trainers ($50 to $120), such as wobble boards and balance balls, help you develop core strength and balance that will prevent injuries.
- Medicine balls ($20 to $75) help you condition your abs and upper body.

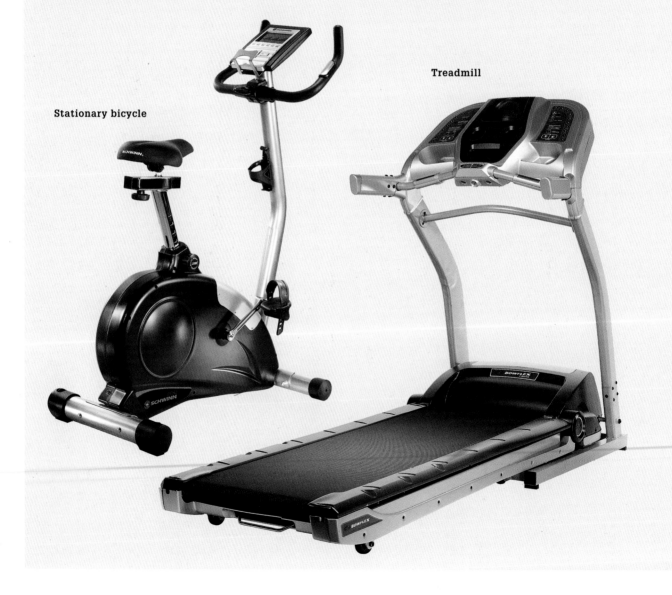

Stationary bicycle

Treadmill

- Free weights (about $1 a pound) can be used in exercises for the entire body.
- Weight benches ($100 to $500) can be fixed or adjustable and may or may not have racks to hold weights or bars. They help you get into position for a variety of lifts.
- Weight machines, also called single-station gyms, ($200 to $3,000 and up) provide stations and weights for strength training. Look for a unit that is designed to fit within the space you have available and one you can add accessories to as you progress in your training.
- Treadmills ($200 to $5,000 and up) come with every bell and whistle you can imagine and a few you probably can't. Whether or not you want a TV with DVD player built into the control panel is strictly a personal issue, but other features are easier to define. You want a unit that runs quietly. It needs to be designed to protect your knees by absorbing as much shock as possible, and the belt should be durable. The motor needs to be reliable and heavy enough to stand up to the weight of its users.
- Elliptical trainers ($500 to $4,000 and up) duplicate walking or running but without impact on your joints. The egg shaped (elliptical) motion takes a little getting used to, but once you get the hang of it, it can be like walking on air. The arms let you work out your upper body along with your legs. Key features include a smooth motion and durable mechanisms.

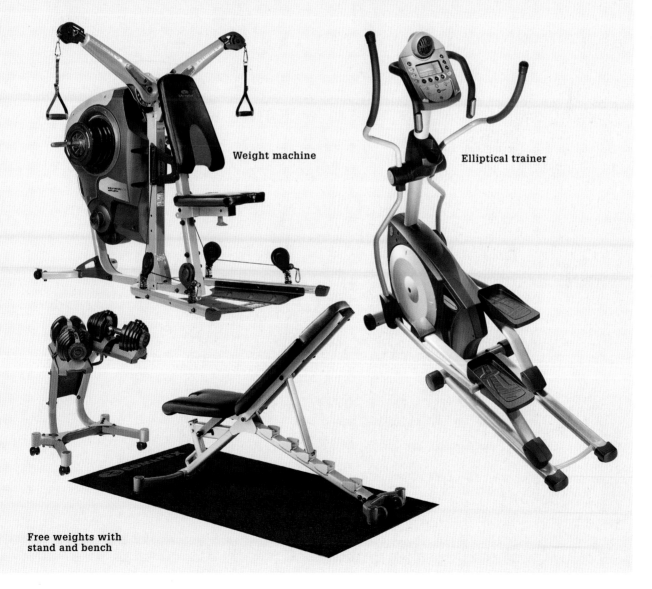

Weight machine

Elliptical trainer

Free weights with stand and bench

Home Office

Whether it's primarily used for running a business or paying personal bills, a home office is a more productive setting if it's separated from everyday household traffic and noise. In a basement, the wide-open space is ideal for creating a large, formal office, but a quiet corner can be perfect for a small work station. Walkout basements are especially suitable for offices that receive visitors and clients, because they have their own outside entrances. You can add signage or landscape around the entrance to give it a professional appearance. But be sure to check the zoning requirements in your area regarding public office space.

Keep in mind that basement offices need plenty of lighting. An office that's too dark will be unappealing—to you and to clients. If possible, plan your office around an existing window, or add a window for more natural light. If the office has no windows, use abundant ambient lighting to give the room a general sense of warmth.

Planning a basement office that works for you involves many factors, including determining the best layout for your needs, ensuring comfort over long hours of work, and providing the necessary hookups for your equipment.

Electrical Needs ▸

It's a good idea to have access to one or more new circuits that serve only your home office equipment. This will reduce the chances of downtimes caused by circuit overloads. To determine how much power is needed for your equipment, add up the amperage (amps) drawn by all of the pieces. The amps should be listed on the back of each device. The total number of amps used on one circuit should not exceed 80% of the circuit's rating. Install enough receptacles to accommodate the devices you currently have, as well as a few extras for equipment you may need in the future.

Also make sure you have all the communications wiring you'll need—for Internet access, fax machines, business and personal phone lines, etc. As with the electrical outlets, including extra wiring and jacks now may be far more convenient and cost effective than adding them later.

A home office needn't be elaborate. If it's thoughtfully designed, even the smallest area can be an efficient workspace. Nor does a home office necessarily need its own room. In shared spaces, however, everyone will feel more comfortable if there is some sense of division or an implied boundary, such as a standing screen, curtain, bookcase, or lowered ceiling.

Office Layouts ▸

These typical office layouts can help you find a configuration that will work for your given space. To help with your planning, think about the tasks you do most often and how much storage space you'll need for commonly used materials. Approximate sizes are given for each typical office element.

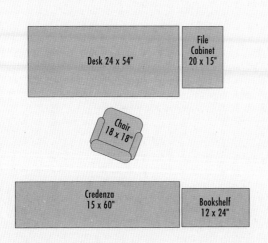

Wall Layout. With this simple layout, the desk and storage units are aligned along one wall. Although this is a good choice for offices with limited space, it is less efficient than other arrangements because the elements are not always within easy reach.

Parallel Layout. In this arrangement, there are two desks or tables set a few feet apart from each other with a chair in between. A parallel layout makes it easy to separate your work by task; for example, you can set your computer on one surface and place your files and phone on the other.

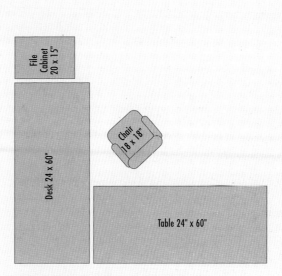

L-shaped Layout. This configuration is the most effective for a corner. You can also use it to divide a space, by placing one leg of the L against a wall and letting the other leg project out into the room. The L shape gives you fairly easy access to a large work surface.

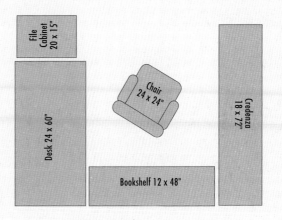

U-shaped Layout. This layout creates the most efficient work area because all of the elements are within easy reach. By adding a chair on the outside of one of the work surfaces, you can create a small conference area.

Built-in Bar

Owning your own basement bar makes a statement about you. For some, it might say "I have arrived and this is my space!" While for others a bar might say "Welcome, friends, our home is your home." And for others, well, let's just say the possibilities are fairly wide ranging. But whatever story your bar tells—be it one of quiet aperitifs before dining, casual afternoons watching the big game, or raucous evenings of wild revelry—building your basement bar yourself personalizes the tale and adds a feature to your home that will have a direct impact on how well you enjoy your home life.

The bar shown here is sleekly styled and smartly laid out for the efficient barkeeper. A small refrigerator gives you access to cold drinks and ice while convenient cabinets create excellent storage spots for party favors.

While this is a dry bar (no plumbing), the design could be modified in any number of ways to add running water if you wish. All you need to get the party started is a GFCI electrical outlet and the proper floor space.

This compact corner bar design features glossy black MDF aprons with decorative cherry appliqués forming a horizontal grid pattern on the aprons. A cherry plywood bartop sits atop a 2 x 6 L-shaped kneewall, harboring some practical amenities on the bartender side. A flip-up lift gate in the bartop on one end provides pass-through access and can even function as a wait station if you want to get really fancy in your hosting

The key components—base cabinets, a laminate countertop, the fridge, and the wood for a sleek Asian-inspired style trim-out—set the stage for your next gathering.

A basement lounge means basically one thing: A bar. Whether it's a wet bar (with plumbing) or dry, a clubby or retro feeling is right at home.

Cutaway View

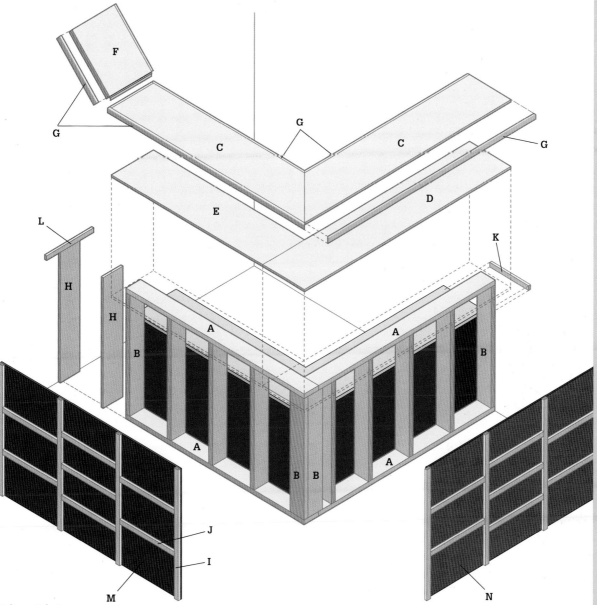

Cutting List

Part	Qty.	Desc.	Size	Material
A	4	Sill/header	$1\frac{1}{2} \times 5\frac{1}{2} \times 68"$	2 × 6
B	11	Stud	$1\frac{1}{2} \times 5\frac{1}{2} \times 38"$	2 × 6
C	2	Bartop	$\frac{3}{4} \times 16\frac{1}{2} \times 80"$	Cherry plywood
D	1	Bar substrate	$\frac{3}{4} \times 16\frac{1}{2} \times 80"$	Particleboard
E	1	Bar substrate	$\frac{3}{4} \times 16\frac{1}{2} \times 65\frac{1}{4}"$	Particleboard
F	2	Lift gate	$\frac{3}{4} \times 16\frac{1}{2} \times 22\frac{1}{4}"$	Cherry plywood
G	6	Bartop trim	$\frac{3}{4} \times 1\frac{1}{2}" \times$ cut to fit	Cherry

Part	Qty.	Desc.	Size	Material
H	2	End cap	$\frac{3}{4} \times 7\frac{3}{4} \times 41"$	Cherry
I	7	Trim stiles	$\frac{3}{4} \times 1\frac{1}{2} \times 41"$	Cherry
J	16	Trim rails	$\frac{3}{4} \times 1\frac{1}{2} \times$ cut to fit	Cherry
K	1	Countertop cleat	$1\frac{1}{2} \times 1\frac{1}{2} \times 22"$	2 × 2
L	1	Lift gate stop block	$\frac{3}{4} \times 1\frac{1}{2} \times 18"$	Cherry
M	1	Apron	$\frac{1}{2} \times 40\frac{1}{2} \times 68\frac{3}{4}"$	MDF
N	1	Apron	$\frac{1}{2} \times 40\frac{1}{2} \times 68\frac{3}{4}"$	MDF

How to Build a Built-In Bar

1

Install walls and flooring and then begin installing the built-in bar. The bar shown here is made using principles taken from both frame carpentry and trim carpentry. The walls of the bar are essentially stub walls that meet at a 90° angle. Use pressure treated 2 x 6 to make the sole plates. Attach the plates with construction adhesive and screws if there is a subfloor, or use a powder-actuated tool.

2

Toenail 2 x 6 corner studs to the sole plate after you have joined the three pieces together into a U-shaped assembly. Attach another 2 x 6 to the wall at the closed end of the bar. If the 2 x 6 is not over a stud location, remove wall coverings, install a cross block nailer in the stud cavity, and then repair the wall. Check with a level to make sure all studs are plumb.

3

Install the reaming 2 x 6 stud (roughly 16" on-center) and then cap the rails that butt together at the corner.

4

Make the apron panels. Here, ½" medium density fiberboard (MDF) is used. Coat the panels with glossy black paint. For best results, use an HVLP sprayer and finish the panels in a separate, well-ventilated room.

Set one apron panel onto a ¼"-thick spacer next to the stub walls and position it. Attach it to the stub wall with construction adhesive and finish nails.

Position and nail the second apron panel into place, driving nails at 8 to 10" intervals. Because you will be attaching corner molding, don't worry too much about small gaps where the aprons meet.

Install the particleboard subbase for the countertop. Butt the strips together, centering them on the stub wall cap rails. Fasten them with construction adhesive and deck screws. Be sure to countersink the screwheads slightly.

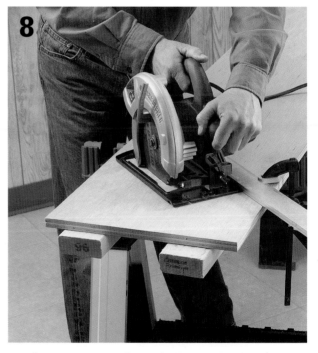

Cut the countertop strips to size from quality cherry-veneer plywood. The two mating ends should be mitered. Double-check the subbase corner to make sure it is exactly 90° (use a carpenter's square). If it is not, miter-cut the first panel at 45°, set it in place, and measure the remaining angle. Cut the second strip to that angle.

(continued)

Fasten the cherry plywood countertop sections to the subbase by driving 1¼" wallboard screws up through the subbase and into the countertops. Countersink the screwheads but not so much that they penetrate the veneer layer.

Attach strips of solid cherry edging to the edges of the countertop. If you're handy with a router, cut a roundover profile on one edge of each strip (the edge that faces away form the countertop. Use adhesive and 4d casing nails driven into pilot holes to attach the edging.

Cut an end panel to fit over the open end of the stub wall beneath the countertop edging. Attach with adhesive and 4d nails driven through pilot holes. Make sure the panel is wide enough to conceal the edges of the apron panel and the ends of the decorative apron strips that will be installed later.

Attach another cherry end panel and a 1 x 2 cherry stop block to the wall to create a resting spot for the hinged portion of the countertop (called the lift gate) when it is in the down position. Use wall anchors instead of nails if the block is not at a stud location (or, cut open the wall and install a cross block nailer).

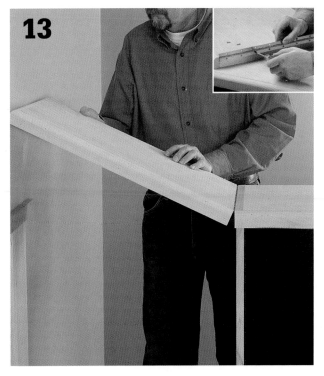

Install the lift gate. Build the lift gate from two pieces of cherry plywood sandwiched together, each with its good face out, and install cherry edging all around. Attach a piano hinge (inset) to the lift gate first and then to the end of the countertop. Test the hinge action.

Attach the decorative cherry trim strips to the aprons in a ladder pattern. Use finish nails and adhesive to attach them. For maximum efficiency, rip-cut all your trim stock on a table saw and then sand and finish the strips as a group (inset) before cutting them to final length.

Install base cabinets behind the bar for storage. A postform countertop is a convenient touch. Create an opening for a minifridge by attaching a cleat to the wall at the closed end of the bar.

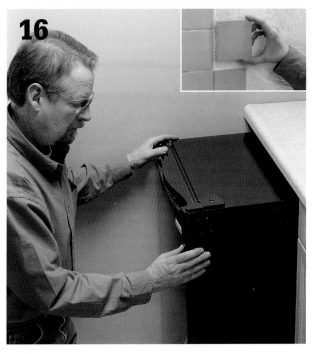

Slide the minifridge into the opening beneath the countertop and plug it in. If you are bothered by the exposed portion of the stub wall above the countertop, create a tile backsplash to conceal it (inset).

Conversion Charts

Metric Conversions

To Convert:	To:	Multiply by:
Inches	Millimeters	25.4
Inches	Centimeters	2.54
Feet	Meters	0.305
Yards	Meters	0.914
Square inches	Square centimeters	6.45
Square feet	Square meters	0.093
Square yards	Square meters	0.836
Ounces	Milliliters	30.0
Pints (U.S.)	Liters	0.473 (Imp. 0.568)
Quarts (U.S.)	Liters	0.946 (Imp. 1.136)
Gallons (U.S.)	Liters	3.785 (Imp. 4.546)
Ounces	Grams	28.4
Pounds	Kilograms	0.454

To Convert:	To:	Multiply by:
Millimeters	Inches	0.039
Centimeters	Inches	0.394
Meters	Feet	3.28
Meters	Yards	1.09
Square centimeters	Square inches	0.155
Square meters	Square feet	10.8
Square meters	Square yards	1.2
Milliliters	Ounces	.033
Liters	Pints (U.S.)	2.114 (Imp. 1.76)
Liters	Quarts (U.S.)	1.057 (Imp. 0.88)
Liters	Gallons (U.S.)	0.264 (Imp. 0.22)
Grams	Ounces	0.035
Kilograms	Pounds	2.2

Converting Temperatures

Convert degrees Fahrenheit (F) to degrees Celsius (C) by following this simple formula: Subtract 32 from the Fahrenheit temperature reading. Then, multiply that number by $\frac{5}{9}$. For example, 77°F - 32 = 45. 45 × $\frac{5}{9}$ = 25°C.

To convert degrees Celsius to degrees Fahrenheit, multiply the Celsius temperature reading by $\frac{9}{5}$. Then, add 32. For example, 25°C × $\frac{9}{5}$ = 45. 45 + 32 = 77°F.

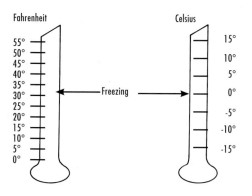

Metric Plywood Panels

Metric plywood panels are commonly available in two sizes: 1,200 mm × 2,400 mm and 1,220 mm × 2,400 mm, which is roughly equivalent to a 4 × 8-ft. sheet. Standard and Select sheathing panels come in standard thicknesses, while Sanded grade panels are available in special thicknesses.

Standard Sheathing Grade		Sanded Grade	
7.5 mm	(⁵⁄₁₆ in.)	6 mm	(⁴⁄₁₇ in.)
9.5 mm	(³⁄₈ in.)	8 mm	(⁵⁄₁₆ in.)
12.5 mm	(½ in.)	11 mm	(⁷⁄₁₆ in.)
15.5 mm	(⅝ in.)	14 mm	(⁹⁄₁₆ in.)
18.5 mm	(¾ in.)	17 mm	(⅔ in.)
20.5 mm	(¹³⁄₁₆ in.)	19 mm	(¾ in.)
22.5 mm	(⅞ in.)	21 mm	(¹³⁄₁₆ in.)
25.5 mm	(1 in.)	24 mm	(¹⁵⁄₁₆ in.)

Lumber Dimensions

Nominal - U.S.	Actual - U.S. (in inches)	Metric
1 × 2	¾ × 1½	19 × 38 mm
1 × 3	¾ × 2½	19 × 64 mm
1 × 4	¾ × 3½	19 × 89 mm
1 × 5	¾ × 4½	19 × 114 mm
1 × 6	¾ × 5½	19 × 140 mm
1 × 7	¾ × 6¼	19 × 159 mm
1 × 8	¾ × 7¼	19 × 184 mm
1 × 10	¾ × 9¼	19 × 235 mm
1 × 12	¾ × 11¼	19 × 286 mm
1¼ × 4	1 × 3½	25 × 89 mm
1¼ × 6	1 × 5½	25 × 140 mm
1¼ × 8	1 × 7¼	25 × 184 mm
1¼ × 10	1 × 9¼	25 × 235 mm
1¼ × 12	1 × 11¼	25 × 286 mm
1½ × 4	1¼ × 3½	32 × 89 mm
1½ × 6	1¼ × 5½	32 × 140 mm
1½ × 8	1¼ × 7¼	32 × 184 mm
1½ × 10	1¼ × 9¼	32 × 235 mm
1½ × 12	1¼ × 11¼	32 × 286 mm
2 × 4	1½ × 3½	38 × 89 mm
2 × 6	1½ × 5½	38 × 140 mm
2 × 8	1½ × 7¼	38 × 184 mm
2 × 10	1½ × 9¼	38 × 235 mm
2 × 12	1½ × 11¼	38 × 286 mm
3 × 6	2½ × 5½	64 × 140 mm
4 × 4	3½ × 3½	89 × 89 mm
4 × 6	3½ × 5½	89 × 140 mm

Liquid Measurement Equivalents

1 Pint	= 16 Fluid Ounces	= 2 Cups
1 Quart	= 32 Fluid Ounces	= 2 Pints
1 Gallon	= 128 Fluid Ounces	= 4 Quarts

Drill Bit Guide

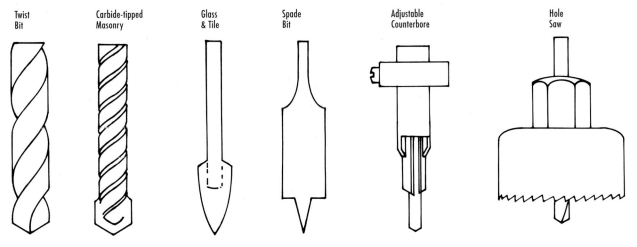

Twist Bit   Carbide-tipped Masonry   Glass & Tile   Spade Bit   Adjustable Counterbore   Hole Saw

Nails

Nail lengths are identified by numbers from 4 to 60 followed by the letter "d," which stands for "penny." For general framing and repair work, use common or box nails. Common nails are best suited to framing work where strength is important. Box nails are smaller in diameter than common nails, which makes them easier to drive and less likely to split wood. Use box nails for light work and thin materials. Most common and box nails have a cement or vinyl coating that improves their holding power.

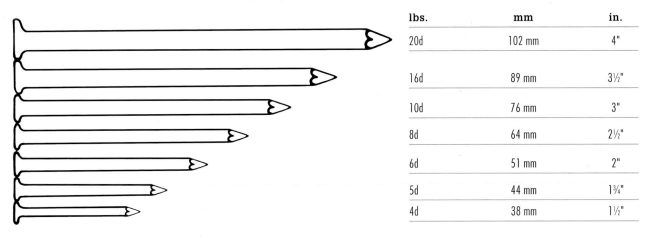

lbs.	mm	in.
20d	102 mm	4"
16d	89 mm	3½"
10d	76 mm	3"
8d	64 mm	2½"
6d	51 mm	2"
5d	44 mm	1¾"
4d	38 mm	1½"

Counterbore, Shank & Pilot Hole Diameters

Screw Size	Counterbore Diameter for Screw Head (in inches)	Clearance Hole for Screw Shank (in inches)	Pilot Hole Diameter Hard Wood (in inches)	Pilot Hole Diameter Soft Wood (in inches)
#1	.146 (9/64)	5/64	3/64	1/32
#2	1/4	3/32	3/64	1/32
#3	1/4	7/64	1/16	3/64
#4	1/4	1/8	1/16	3/64
#5	1/4	1/8	5/64	1/16
#6	5/16	9/64	3/32	5/64
#7	5/16	5/32	3/32	5/64
#8	3/8	11/64	1/8	3/32
#9	3/8	11/64	1/8	3/32
#10	3/8	3/16	1/8	7/64
#11	1/2	3/16	5/32	9/64
#12	1/2	7/32	9/64	1/8

Resources

American Institute of Architects
800-364-9364
www.aiaonline.com

American Society of Interior Designers
202-546-3480
www.asid.org

Apex Custom Wine Cellars
Manufacturer of wine racks and cooling systems;
    featured on p. 13 (lower right), 92
888-999-9749
www.apexwinecellars.com

Armstrong World Industries
Flooring and ceiling tiles; featured on p. 100 to 104
717-397-0611

Association of Home Appliance Manufacturers
202-872-5955
www.aham.org

International Residential Code (book)
International Conference of Building Officials
800-284-4406
www.icbo.com

LATICRETE International Inc.
Manufacturer of radiant floor mats
    featured on pages 86–91
800-243-4788
www.laticrete.com

National Association of the Remodeling Industry
703-575-1100
www.nari.org

National Kitchen & Bath Association (NKBA)
800-843-6522
www.nkba.com

2nd Wind Exercise Equipment
Treadmill featured on p. 106
952-544-5249
www.2ndwind.net

**U.S. Environmental Protection Agency Indoor
    air quality**
www.epa.gov/iedweb00/pubs/insidest.html

Photo Credits

p. 4 Elizabeth Whiting & Associates /
    www.EWAstock.com
p. 6 © Anne Gummerson /
    www.AnneGummersonPhoto.com
p. 8 Elizabeth Whiting Associates / www.EWAstock.com
p. 10 © Beth Singer / www.BethSingerPhotographer.com
p. 11 (top) Elizabeth Whiting & Associates /
    www.EWAstock.com, (lower) Cal Spas
p. 12 (top) Elizabeth Whiting & Associates /
    www.EWAstock.com, (lower left) © Beth Singer /
    www.BethSingerPhotographer.com, (lower right)
    www.iStockPhoto.com
p. 40 (lower left) Courtesy of Dow AgroSciences LLC
    (Sentricon Termite Colony Elimination System)
p. 80 photo courtesy of Room & Board® /
    www.RoomAndBoard.com
p. 100 (left) photo courtesy of Armstrong® /
    www.Armstrong.com (877-276-7876)
p. 110 www.iStockPhoto.com

p. 122 & 164 photo courtesy of Armstrong /
    www.Armstrong.com (877-276-7876)
p. 196 www.iStockPhoto.com
p. 235 (lower right) www.iStockPhoto.com
p. 236 © Eric Roth / www.EricRothPhoto.com
p. 237 (top) photo courtesy of Broan NuTone® /
    www.Broan-Nutone.com (262-673-4340), (lower)
    © Linda Oyama Bryan for Orren Pickell Designers &
    Builders
p. 238 www.iStockPhoto.com / © Michele Malven
p. 239 (top) www.iStockPhoto.com / © Sandra O'Claire
p. 240 to 241 (all) photos courtesy of Nautilus /
    www.Nautilus.com
p. 242 photo courtesy of California Closets® /
    www.CaliforniaClosets.com

Index

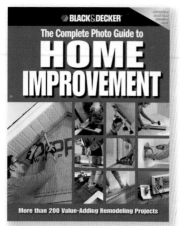

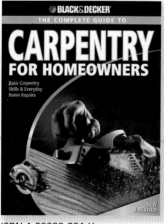